# THE PERIL OF
# MODERNIZING JESUS

# THE PERIL OF MODERNIZING JESUS

By

Henry J. Cadbury

*Wipf & Stock*
PUBLISHERS
*Eugene, Oregon*

Wipf and Stock Publishers
199 W 8th Ave, Suite 3
Eugene, OR 97401

The Peril of Modernizing Jesus
By Cadbury, Henry J.
Copyright©1937 Estate of Henry J. Cadbury
ISBN 13: 978-1-55635-145-7
ISBN 10: 1-55635-145-3
Publication date: 1/9/2006
Previously published by The Macmillan Co., 1937

# FOREWORD TO THE 2007 EDITION

As one of the leading figures in producing the Revised Standard Version of the Bible, Henry Joel Cadbury did much of the translation work himself. On occasion, when callers stopped by asking to see the Harvard professor, Mrs. Cadbury would declare: "I'm sorry, Henry cannot be disturbed just now; he's upstairs rewriting the Word of God!" Indeed, the tendency of interpreters is to fill in the gaps where the biblical text is silent, or to skip over the awkward passages if not conducive to contemporary readers. Cadbury, however, fought long and hard to preserve the plain and simple diction of the Bible, even if that meant adding to our problems as interpreters. None of his subjects exemplified this passion for preserving the meaning of the unadorned text more than his treatments of Jesus, and the third printing of his first book on Jesus is as relevant today as it was nearly seven decades ago.

First published in 1937, *The Peril of Modernizing Jesus* broke against the grain in North American and European New Testament studies.[1] For one thing, it challenged what

---

[1] Appreciation is expressed to the Cadbury family for granting the permission to publish this book, as well as to the Macmillan Company for its original publishing of Cadbury's

*Foreword*

Cadbury would later call "the eclipse of the historical Jesus" in the wake of Albert Schweitzer's epoch-making coverage of Jesus scholarship from Reimarus to Wrede.[2] In this book Cadbury challenges the view that virtually nothing can be known of the Jesus of history, punctuating the Jesus-studies landscape between the "No Quest" sealed by Schweitzer and the "New Quest" inaugurated by Bornkamm. A good deal can be known about Jesus, even if it involves information about a leading rural figure in ancient Palestine.

On the other hand, Cadbury's book also challenges our tendencies to sketch a portrait of Jesus created in our image as modernists. Did Jesus really have a programmatic goal, or did he respond primarily to occasional needs? Was Jesus interested in changing society as a social reformer, or was he an apocalyptist envisioning God's sovereign fulfillment of history? Was Jesus really a salesman trying to gain adherents, or was he an apologist for truth and authenticity? Did Jesus have a set of teachings to propound, or was he primarily interested in responsive obedience to the divine will? In these ways and others, Cadbury challenges incisively our modern interests in relevance at the expense of sober historical-critical analysis.

---

Lowell Lectures delivered in Boston in 1935.

[2] Cadbury's Haverford Library Lectures were published as Pendle Hill Pamphlet #133 as *The Eclipse of the Historical Jesus*, Wallingford, PA: Pendle Hill Publications (1963).

*Foreword*

One of the reasons for this set of critical challenges was the tendency for experts in related fields to offer relevant information in hopes of eliminating the vacuum left in the wake of Schweitzer's deconstructive challenge. As one reviewer put it:

> While within the past generation the old-fashioned devotional "lives of Christ" have been less frequently written, they have been replaced by a constantly increasing flood of books by specialists in other fields than historical theology. When a scholar has attained competence in (say) sociology, economics, ethics, pedagogy, psychology in general or religious psychology in particular, he often feels that he has thus attained the key to the "Jesus problem" and sets forth his conclusions in print.[3]

On these inclinations, Cadbury's contribution is similar to that of Schweitzer's in that it challenges the supplanting of both the Christ of faith and the Jesus of history with "the Jesus of Modernism." And yet, Cadbury also extends a sympathetic hand to the modernizer, in that our interests in finding meaning in first-century gospel narratives will always lend themselves to making connections between the ministry of Jesus and the needs of our world today. "Anachronism in thinking about Jesus," says Cadbury, "has been largely due to an excusable ignorance.

---

[3] Burton Scott Easton, review of *The Peril of Modernizing Jesus* by Henry J. Cadbury, Anglican Theological Review 20 (1938) 143–44.

*Foreword*

The gospels do not give us all the information we need, especially for the inner life of Jesus" (p. 28). Nonetheless, the tendency to fill in the gaps must be resisted by those endeavoring to make adequate inroads into understanding the Jesus of history.

As perilous as is modernizing Jesus, however, is the tendency to archaize ourselves, and Cadbury addressed that problem as well.[4] Is the best way to make connections with the Jesus of Galilee to emulate his diet, his dress, and all of his religious teachings? After all, Jesus was a first-century Galilean Jew, and it would be several generations before the religious movement founded in his memory became individuated from Judaism. As Cadbury later said, "The modernizer carelessly paints Moses in Oxford shoes, or the Virgin with a wrist watch. The archaizer will deliberately adopt the sandals, the phylacteries, and the whole garb both inner and outer of the biblical era. . . . The archaizer mistakes the portrait for a mirror while the other mistakes the mirror for a portrait."[5]

While much of the thrust of this book is deconstructive, it also builds and emphasizes important historical considerations about the Jesus of history that are highly relevant for later cultures and times. First, he emphasizes the Jewishness of the gospels and Jesus. As an apocalyptic and "unmodern" prophetic figure, Jesus'

---

[4] "The Peril of Archaizing Ourselves," *Interpretation* 3 (1949) 331–38.

[5] Ibid.

*Foreword*

worldview as an "ancient theist" was very different from our notions of natural law and cause-effect relationships today. Rather, God's direct involvement in the playing out of worldly events, whether they be the ushering in of God's kingdom or deliverance from physical illness and demonic oppression, was likely assumed by Jesus. This would have been the case with any first-century Jewish leader, and Jesus' interest in partnering with God in the carrying out of the divine will personally seems to have taken precedence over programmatic notions of what that might involve.

It is at this point that Cadbury's work will likely be the most challenging for the modern interpreter seeking to further an understanding of societal reform patterned after the works and teachings of Jesus. Just as Cadbury had elsewhere emphasized the informality of early Christianity in terms of its structures for organization and forms of worship,[6] here he challenges social reformers as to the degree to which Jesus can rightly be yoked to our causes, and even helpful social programs. While Jesus' words and works still speak to us today, we must confess that there is much we do not know, and we must acknowledge that we ourselves are involved in the making of meaning.

---

[6] See one of his first essays, "Christianity in the Making," *Present Day Papers* 2 (1915) 58–61; and his later essay, "The Informality of Early Christianity," *Crozer Quarterly* 21 (1944) 246–55.

*Foreword*

In some ways Cadbury might overstep his bounds in criticizing what cannot be known about Jesus' mission and ministry.[7] For instance, how do we really know that he wasn't interested in changing the world? He certainly sent his disciples out to be healers, exorcists, and proclaimers of the gospel. And an all-too-easy fallacy tends to be committed by modern positivism, of which Cadbury was a leading proponent among biblical scholars. Assuming that "not necessarily so" implies "necessarily not so" is just as fallacious as its corrected counterpart. The way forward begins with acknowledging the limitations of our knowledge, including a helpful describing of the gradations of our certainty and why. This replaces projection with authoritative analysis, and it also makes for profitable interpretation in sometimes surprising ways.

While Cadbury's criticisms of our modernist tendencies as gospel interpreters might be disturbing to some, they actually call us back to the center of the quest, which is to know something of the authentic mission and message of Jesus. Indeed, the New Quest for the Historical Jesus took off in the 1950s precisely where Cadbury's first Jesus book left off: emphasizing the religious experience and concerns of Jesus as a place to begin our historical inquiry. Of course, whether our investigations lead us

---

[7] This was an insightful criticism in the review by Raymond E. Brewer, *Journal of Bible and Religion* 6 (1938) 92–94, where he raises questions about how it is known that Jesus was less than conscious about grades of selfishness, social motives, or laws of character.

*Foreword*

to the Jesus of history or the Jesus of modernism is a question yet to be decided. Yet any worthy "translation" project begins with distinguishing between the content and its packaging, and that's precisely what Cadbury's book on Jesus helps us do. This book is a must-read for all followers of Jesus studies—modern and postmodern alike!

Paul N. Anderson
George Fox University, 2006

# PREFACE

HEREWITH is offered to a wider audience the substance of some lectures delivered in the spring of 1935 at King's Chapel, Boston, under the auspices of the Lowell Institute. A few quotations have been added either illustrating or condemning the faults of modernization. These could have been multiplied indefinitely. Other aspects of Jesus could also have been chosen for like treatment, but further expansion seemed unnecessary. What is presented is intended to be typical of a general warning. I had hoped that the warning would be given by others before now and so had delayed publication, in the case of some parts of the lectures for ten or twelve years. What is said seems, however, to need saying in some form like the present volume.

The text of the book sufficiently explains its purpose —not to give a rounded portrait of the historical Jesus but rather some hints for correcting our modern way of looking at him. To see Jesus as he was we need to neutralize the bias of our eyes. When my oculist gives

## Preface

me glasses they are not themselves perfect transmitters. Taken alone they are worse than ordinary window glass. They give twisted views and untrue perspective, but they are intended to match and cancel the defects of my eyes. When the unevenness of the lenses is superimposed upon the inaccuracies of the eyes more perfect vision results.

So the following chapters are intended to give, not the object itself, but the means of more accurate vision. By themselves they are doubtless inaccurate and out of perspective; they will not be used alone, however, but will be added to our own modern views and preconceptions. They should be judged only so and not as though they were a complete and independent picture. Who will deny that in looking at the Jesus of history the modern eye needs a corrective that will counter some of the difference between his age and our age, and between his thoughts and our thoughts?

Henry J. Cadbury

Cambridge
Massachusetts

# CONTENTS

| CHAPTER | PAGE |
|---|---|
| I. ANACHRONISM IN THINKING ABOUT JESUS | 1 |
| II. THE CAUSE AND CURE OF MODERNIZATION | 28 |
| III. THE JEWISHNESS OF THE GOSPELS | 49 |
| IV. JESUS AND THE MENTALITY OF OUR AGE | 67 |
| V. LIMITATIONS OF JESUS' SOCIAL TEACHING | 86 |
| VI. PURPOSE, AIM AND MOTIVE IN JESUS | 120 |
| VII. THE RELIGION OF JESUS | 154 |
| NOTES | 194 |
| INDEX | 213 |

Chapter I

# ANACHRONISM IN THINKING ABOUT JESUS

PROBABLY no one has looked even superficially at the paintings on Biblical subjects by great masters without commenting to himself on certain details which did not satisfy even his most amateurish antiquarian sense. Beside the foreground of the main theme, satisfying in line and color as well as in human interest and feeling, there are always little details of background which belong too obviously to the artist's own time and country. The Italian campagna or the polders of Holland plainly can make no claim to Palestinian verisimilitude. Anachronisms of costume and of furnishings soon disclose themselves to a hypercritical eye and with them an absence often of appropriate oriental flora and fauna. Here is Adam in a scene which for all its luxuriance is an obviously Flemish garden of Eden. There is Mary Magdalene with a Florentine headdress. Delilah's embossed silver shears are not of her age or of ours; but in the same museum [1] which displays the picture of her with the sleeping Samson you will find real scissors just like them in a room furnished for the very century of the artist's own lifetime. You can verify the relation by comparing the "period" tapestries with those in Delilah's house. Gross anachronisms are usually avoided, but little ones are not. Perhaps they are sufficient actually to assist the connoisseur to date and place with a fair degree of accuracy canvases of otherwise unknown origin.

These phenomena are not artistic blemishes. They are unobtrusive, especially to the artist's own generation. The great theme with its human or religious interest is unspoiled by them. They are either unthought of, or deliberately accepted. The painter adopts certain conventional features; the rest he draws to life as he knows it. His imagination is active, but its activity does not take the form of scientific archaeological reconstruction. What should Rembrandt know of the exact appearance of first century Jerusalem? Efforts at historical and local fidelity would have seemed to his contemporaries grotesque and outlandish. It was enough that he sought the spirit of the scriptural theme and that he portrayed that with reality. Reality would mean contemporary human lifelikeness, not fidelity to ages long past and to lands unvisited and unknown.

The tendency to make the Bible contemporary with ourselves affects our thinking and speech as it affects

CHAP. I  *Anachronism in Thinking about Jesus*

our art. Local and archaic trustworthiness is the aim as rarely of the theologian or the preacher as of the artist. A more immediate practical objective is in view than education in archaeological accuracy. The modernization is usually unconscious, unobtrusive and inoffensive. The grosser forms of inaccuracy are usually avoided. The uses of gunpowder, steam and electricity enter our Biblical thinking as little as they enter Biblical art. We realize that the paralytic's "bed" was not a four-poster, though artists have not hesitated to use the latter in other subjects. We know in spite of high-backed chairs in pictures of the Last Supper that to "sit at meat" meant to recline. We catch ourselves modernizing Jesus' home and stop to correct ourselves, but there are other anachronisms that almost escape us, as when a recent writer talks of "Jesus' bookshelf" or when we think of reading or writing in terms of modern book forms or even of a modern European language.

Far more important is it to realize that what we do with Jesus' clothes or setting we do, perhaps more unconsciously and therefore with less restraint, with Jesus' mind. For the patterns of thought change as do the patterns of clothes from land to land and from age to age, and the thoughts of a first century Jew like Jesus or Paul are not the thoughts of a twentieth century Englishman or German or American. There are, no doubt, fundamental likenesses of mind, as there are likenesses of the human body, but there are also differences which distinguish not only individuals, but cultures and generations. Possibly our age differs more from Jesus' age in ways of thinking than in ways of living. Manufacture, transportation, communication, we know to be now quite different; but do we realize how different is the outlook we have on life, on duty and on God? Mental processes, intellectual assumptions, forms of selfconsciousness and all the furniture of the mind differ as does the furniture of houses. Perhaps the former change more completely and significantly than the latter. In any case, we are less likely to reconstruct the mental furniture of past ages and cultures, although the materials are not lacking for doing so. Hence we fall into anachronism in thinking of Jesus' thoughts.

The attempt to avoid anachronism cannot be regarded as an easy or self-evident process. "Nothing is more difficult in the study of history," says a church historian, "than to put oneself back into the thoughts and feelings of past centuries, and to view events from a standpoint the very foundations of which have utterly perished."[2] No one who has attempted to write history can be ignorant of the difficulty.

Even quite external and datable facts often creep into the wrong context. One of the commonest errors

CHAP. I  *Anachronism in Thinking about Jesus*

in the life of Jesus is the supposition, perhaps accepted even by Luke, that the darkness of the crucifixion was an eclipse of the sun. But very little reflection and an elementary knowledge of astronomy are required to correct such a suggestion. Whatever the exact day and year, the Friday on which Jesus died was near the passover, the passover was near the full moon, and "solar eclipses can occur only at the time of the new moon."

Less easy is another Biblical problem. The anachronisms in the paintings of Bible scenes have already been mentioned. One of these is a widely reproduced picture of Ruth and Naomi. The two women in the foreground have just separated from Orpah. There is little scenery, but among other things is a bit of cactus or prickly pear so familiar in present day Palestine in hedges and detached plants. To include this ubiquitous though ugly weed was no doubt intended by the painter as a piece of local color. But is it also contemporary color? Most botanists would say decisively not. If, as is commonly supposed, the prickly pear was first introduced from Europe into Palestine at the Crusades the painter has committed an anachronism of some two thousand years. Then the Egyptologist comes along and shows us an Egyptian picture of the garden of a Syrian princess as old as the time of Ruth, or even older, and in that ancient picture is without doubt the crude but clear outline of the prickly pear. A cautious man can hardly decide whether the modern painting has an anachronism or not.

Few of us indeed are really sensitive to anachronism. When it is intentional and is broadly obvious, of course we notice it. It is in fact a deliberate and effective tool of humor, as in Mark Twain's *Connecticut Yankee at King Arthur's Court,* or in some of Bernard Shaw's historical plays. Otherwise we easily overlook it. Take for example the film production of Louisa Alcott's *Little Women.* In one of the most attractive scenes during the Civil War, with the father still away at the front, the women folks of the family gather on Christmas eve about the piano—or was it a harpsichord?— and sing:

> O little town of Bethlehem,
> How still we see thee lie!
> Above thy deep and dreamless sleep
> The silent stars go by:
> Yet in thy dark streets shineth
> The everlasting Light;
> The hopes and fears of all the years
> Are met in thee tonight.

This hymn of Phillips Brooks is so familiar to us today, so appropriate to the occasion, that I believe very

CHAP. I   *Anachronism in Thinking about Jesus*

few who see and hear the play realize that it was first written in 1868, four years too late for the Civil War setting, and was in fact not published until 1894.

Even the modern costuming of Biblical characters often passes unnoticed. One would have to be a real expert in the history of jewelry to know how much of the lavish ornaments of a painted Queen of Sheba, or a Mary Magdalene, or of a Virgin Mary is really true to the ancient jeweler's art. I will admit that as a sightseer in the churches of Jerusalem I must have passed over many a glaring anachronism until one day in the Church of the Holy Sepulchre I saw a real wrist watch on the arm of a statue of the Virgin. That at least was an innovation one degree too much. Anachronism there was blatant and absurd. To see a modern timepiece on the modern Arab is strange enough; how much more so with the first century Palestinian peasant woman. I can but recall the surprise of the little girl in the first page of *Alice in Wonderland*, "when the white rabbit actually took a watch out of its waistcoat pocket and looked at it . . . Alice started to her feet for it flashed before her mind that she had never before seen a rabbit with either a waistcoat pocket or a watch to take out of it."

We have compared the external and the internal modernizing of Jesus, but may notice now that the avoidance of the former is no guarantee of avoidance of the latter. The most painstaking historical and geographical study of Jesus' physical environment is not sufficient to prevent the quite careless modernization of his thought. There is a kind of authority implied in scholarly knowledge of his times which often quite wrongly carries over to the reconstruction of his inner life. Historical and geographical study is not to be undervalued on that account, but the necessity for combining with it a sympathy and understanding of the ancient mind is not to be neglected. Two generations ago the fault was well illustrated by Renan's *Vie de Jésus*. Here was a biography, perhaps the first, which was built upon a knowledge of Greek and Semitic civilization that was admirable for its age, but Renan combined with it an inescapable modern sentimentality and rationality that tended to put the inner life of Jesus completely out of historical focus. In more recent times the continuance of patient research and the popular education in the historical and literary study of the gospels has not prevented but rather has encouraged an assured modernism in claiming to have recovered the inner as well as the outer reality of Jesus' career.

Not even the use of Jesus' own terms prevents an almost complete modernizing of him. In fact to use them in a modern sense only deceives ourselves and others into thinking that we are accurately represent-

CHAP. I    *Anachronism in Thinking about Jesus*

ing his ideas. It is doubtful, of course, whether Jesus used a word "gospel" at all, but if he did its content was almost certainly very different from most that goes under its name in any sort of American pulpit. We are doubtless correct in supposing that Jesus called God "father," but that the word was for him pregnant with meanings such as we give it, is not so probable. Terms for God are peculiarly conventional, and human fatherhood, neither then nor today, carries even ideally such concepts as we often read into Jesus' use of it,— of unity of will, and mutual understanding; of loving care on one side and filial dependence on the other. The modern Christian speaks too, after Jesus, of "the Kingdom of God." In how many directions our view of the Kingdom is unlike Jesus' view it would be tedious to enumerate. One difference, however, is particularly clear. For Jesus the Kingdom was nothing that men themselves build or create as for the average modernist. If these frequent and familiar terms of Jesus are used by us to describe our modern humanitarian ideals, our sense of creating a better world, our longing for fellowship and mystical communion with God, how much more likely are we to miss his meaning in other passages.

Examples may be taken almost at random from modern writings. Here is a description of the search for the boy Jesus by his parents:

*The Peril of Modernizing Jesus*     CHAP. I

The crowd of travellers, all homeward bound, was tremendous. . . . The tents were pitched and the roll was called, and Jesus was lost! Nothing could be done that night; but in the early morning, Mary and Joseph hurried off to retrace their steps through the maze of traffic that was now against them. No wonder their journey was slow, too slow altogether for their anxious forebodings! But Jerusalem at last! A hurried search through the morgue, the police stations, the doctors' offices—and then, with a sigh of relief, the sudden appearance of the boy among the great men of the Temple staff, "both hearing and asking them questions." [3]

A book well known in America a few years ago was entitled *The Man Nobody Knows*. It is a very human portrait of Jesus, full of vivid pictures of modern life read into the ancient story. When it paraphrases the gospel account of Jesus' visit to Nazareth it refers to his mother in the kitchen recognizing his footsteps, to his brothers and sisters hastening from other parts of the house to greet him, and finally to his retiring at night upstairs alone to his own old room.[4]

We shall not be surprised if writers who can think of doctors' offices and a morgue in Jerusalem, or of a first century house in Nazareth with a separate kitchen and private upstairs bedrooms for a family of eight or more persons, betray the modernness of their thinking and even their own professions in their account of

CHAP. I  *Anachronism in Thinking about Jesus*

Jesus. Thus in the first cited volume, we are reproachfully asked, "How many of us have ever stopped to picture Jesus, like any modern preacher, in the act of preparing his sermons?"[5]

The other book already mentioned is full, especially in one chapter, of the viewpoint of the advertising expert. For its author Jesus exemplifies all the principles of modern salesmanship. He was, of course, a good mixer; he made contacts easily and was quick to get *en rapport* with his "prospect." He appreciated the advertising value of news and so called his message "good news." His habit of early rising was indicative of the high pressure of the "go-getter" so necessary for a successful career.[6] His experience in the Temple at the age of twelve, already mentioned, reveals to this author how early Jesus has determined upon his profession. It was to be a life not of teaching nor of preaching, but of business: "Wist ye not that I must be about my Father's *business?*"[7]

Such anachronisms are easily detected when attention is called to them, but in other cases, especially the subtler statements which modern writers make concerning Jesus' thought or purpose or insight, while one cannot speak assuredly, one is justified in suspecting that equally unhistorical effects are produced. For example, here is a pedagogical technique attributed to him:

## The Peril of Modernizing Jesus  CHAP. I

His refusal to give plain answers to plain questions—his constant habit of dealing with one question by asking another—was, we should gather, part of a general refusal to teach explicitly and dogmatically, lest he should thereby stunt a man's capacity for finding his own answers to his own question by the light given him within.[8]

The modernizing of Jesus is not always limited to special sections. It sometimes pervades a whole description. Here for example is given as briefly as possible the contents of an article by a distinguished Christian layman, entitled, "The Economic Factor in the Messiahship of Jesus."

Jesus knew that the Jewish people had to grow strong. ... To begin with, there had to be more people. ... How could they produce enough to support a large population? The only answer to that question is that they must develop and utilize the productive capacity of the people to the maximum. This is primarily a problem of economizing human energy, of eliminating every form of waste, especially the waste of human energy, which is the worst form of waste. Idleness, vice, dissipation, suspicion of one another, covetousness or jealousy of success, ostentation, pride, vanity, luxury, quarreling, distraction, and all such things have to be eliminated before any people can achieve its maximum success, because these are all forms of wasted human energy. Good-will, generous appreciation of the achievements of others, self-discipline to the extent of developing all one's powers and applying them to the doing of useful

CHAP. I   *Anachronism in Thinking about Jesus*

or life-supporting things,—these must take the place of the vices or wasteful habits that generally prevail. . . . Our young Jew set out to accomplish these things, knowing that if he succeeded he would be laying the foundations of national freedom. If his people would substitute these constructive virtues for their destructive vices, they would speedily become a great people because they would deserve to be great, and they would achieve their freedom because they were fit to be free.

Other things had to be done before the answer was complete. The old superstitious taboo against interest had to be removed. In the parable of the talents and the pounds he gave us as clear and definite a justification of interest as is contained in any text-book in economics. The episode of the barren fig-tree is a clear lesson in the conservation of land. If good land is cumbered with unfruitful trees, the maximum production could never be reached, and the maximum strength never attained.

It is also a waste to have land or any other productive agent in the hands of a poor manager when it might be in the hands of a better manager. In addition to justifying interest, the story of the talents or the pounds teaches this lesson as clearly as it could be taught. Substitute the word "tool" or the word "acre" for the word "talent" or "pound" and you get a most important economic lesson.[9]

Even to those of us most familiar with the Social Gospel the anachronism of such a presentation must be at sight evident. The reader will not be surprised to learn that the author is an economist of the capitalist

*The Peril of Modernizing Jesus*  CHAP. I

school of laissez-faire and rugged individualism, and that he regards Jesus as "the very opposite of a socialist." "Socialism," he continues, "is essentially pagan and unchristian. Every essential feature of the modern economic system is explicitly set forth in the teachings of this young Jew, who hoped that his own people might profit by them and become a great free people." Equally unhistorical interpretations can be made from the opposite viewpoint. The trouble is not the special theory attributed to Jesus, but the anachronistic way of setting the problem, the misuse of the parables, and the ultra-modern portraiture of Jesus' mind.

So long as our interests are purely practical, modern, and artistic such modernizing of Jesus is not more serious than is the external modernizing of him by the painters. For those who regard Jesus as an historical figure, worth recovering in his actuality, this tendency of ours seems something that deserves attention and correction. Aliens as we are to his time and clime we come in the spirit of those Greeks of whom John's gospel speaks, crying, "We would see Jesus."

There is nothing unique or blameworthy in such an aim. In many circles, including some in which little claim is made of allegiance to him, a feeling prevails that the true character of Jesus has been obscured, while more devout believers have repeated the cry of the Magdalen: "They have taken away my Lord and

CHAP. I   *Anachronism in Thinking about Jesus*

I know not where they have laid him." But the criteria for this correction vary widely. Too often the test is only a different modern preconception, rather than the strict effort at history. Unbiased recovery of history is always a difficult task and nowhere more so than in those events of history to which religious tradition is most intimately attached. The complete apprehension of another mentality is scarcely to be expected without some error. According to Spengler one can never understand another culture. He is presumptuous who claims a lack of bias or promises success. Yet we know something of what historical method should be, and can offer even in controversial areas certain suggestions of the kind of corrective that our thinking about Jesus requires, if we are not to fall into errors of anachronism.

These pages do not aim at a new life of Jesus. Such lives are needed and, as has already been suggested, they are being attempted. Many of the old portraits are not faithful to the original. But the new lives confuse reality with modernness and substitute a more modern and hence less conspicuous bias for the traditional unrealities. The titles of some recent books are characteristic—*The Man Nobody Knows, The Rediscovery of Jesus, The Real Jesus, Our Recovery of Jesus, The Jesus of History, The Renaissance of Jesus, The Historic Jesus, The Original Jesus, Discovering Jesus.*

*The Peril of Modernizing Jesus*  CHAP. I

All these nine titles occur in the latest five-year catalogue of American publications, expressing a present day self-confidence in our superiority to our predecessors. These books often grow out of unsatisfied modern human need rather than out of painstaking effort to recover from a distant and foreign scene an actual and unidealized fact. At first the processes seem identical, but in the end they differ. One may well ponder again and again those words of Schweitzer, near the close of his influential book, *The Quest of the Historical Jesus:*

> The historical Jesus will be to our time a stranger and an enigma. The study of the Life of Jesus has had a curious history. It set out in quest of the historical Jesus believing that when it had found Him it could bring Him straight into our time as a Teacher and Saviour. It loosed the bands by which He had been riveted for centuries to the stony rocks of ecclesiastical doctrine, and rejoiced to see life and movement coming into the figure once more, and the historical Jesus advancing, as it seemed, to meet it. But He does not stay; He passes by our time and returns to His own.[10]

Perhaps I may conclude with a few illustrations of how the gospels themselves display the tendency of reading later ideas into the record. Significantly, and from one point of view fortunately, for a long period

CHAP. I  *Anachronism in Thinking about Jesus*

of time men did not try to write the life of Christ. Whatever faults the theological prepossession of Christianity from the second century to the eighteenth may have had, few persons were really interested in recovering or knowing the historical Jesus. How many realize that lives of Christ were not written at all during all those years, except the fantastic apocrypha in the early time, and the miracle plays and gospel paraphrases in the middle ages. A life of Christ in the modern sense comes first almost in the nineteenth century.

Although through all this time men were no doubt thinking of Christ in their own image—as a martyr, or a theologian, or a mystic, or an ascetic, or an ecclesiastic—they wrote no full-length biography. If we wish, then, to see the tendency of our times extensively illustrated in a quite different age, we naturally turn to the gospels.

The modernization of Jesus must have begun almost immediately in Christian circles. The situation that followed his death created perspectives that were quite different from those of his lifetime. He was not present in person and three substitutes supplied the new vacancy with equivalents. There was the memory of the past, the hope of his future return, and the present consciousness of the Holy Spirit. The Christian movement had passed into new phases. Its message that

Jesus was the Messiah who had died and risen required confirmation, partly because of inner doubts and partly because of external criticism. It found itself increasingly set apart. It was beset with attacks more vigorous than verbal criticism, with persecution and martyrdom. The Judaism out of which it sprang was hostile. The lines between the synagogue and the church began to be drawn. Unexpected success, however, attended the preaching of Jesus in other circles. Converts were won who were pagan in background and Greek in language. The movement had increasing definiteness of group life. Formal practices like baptism and the Supper and a necessary leadership became customary. Between Christian individuals and groups variety arose, usually unconscious of conflict but sometimes coming into open expression and schism.

These developments could hardly fail to affect the perspective of believers towards Jesus, and our earliest records reflect the new viewpoint. The influence on the synoptic gospels is, however, not so conspicuous as in some other literature of the same time and that for several reasons. There was a fundamental unity in historical setting between Jesus and the evangelists. Their general religious beliefs, their old-world assumptions, their outlook on life were, except in such ways as I have mentioned, almost identical with those of Jesus and his associates. Further, the gospels are based on

CHAP. I   *Anachronism in Thinking about Jesus*

older material, written and oral, which was often allowed to remain unchanged. Above all, the synoptic gospels are so objective in presentation that the kind of modernizing to which special reference has been made, the modernizing of Jesus' inner self, scarcely could come to expression at all.

In spite of these factors, tending as they do to commend the fidelity of the gospel portrait, the gospels almost certainly disclose the influence of their later date. The earthly life of Jesus is not something still in progress but a *fait accompli*. It is looked back to as past history. His words are matters of memory. The earliest formula was "remember the words of the Lord Jesus how he said . . ."[11] It was as past words of present value that they are collected and recorded. Their very wording indicates their value to that later age, so that Jesus himself also reminds them, "Behold I have told you beforehand."

Thus the anticipatory element in Jesus' teaching plays a conspicuous part in the gospels, and the anticipation includes not only Jesus' expectation of his own fate, but that of the disciples in later days, future missionary enterprise, future persecutions, and the whole apocalyptic program. In the latter not Jesus' return but the conduct of the disciples is central. Their sufferings, their temptation to be led astray, their disappointment at hope deferred, their subjection to human maltreatment or their terror at divine portents, their readiness for the final crisis—such are the themes of much of the gospel matter.

The contrast between Jesus' lifetime and the period of the gospels is plainly indicated in several directions in the gospel text.

> So long as they have the bridegroom with them they shall not fast but the days will come when the bridegroom is taken away, in that day they shall fast.
>
> The days will come when ye shall desire to see one of the days of the Son of Man but ye shall not see it.
>
> When I sent you forth without purse and wallet and shoes, lacked ye anything? And they said, Nothing. And he said unto them, But now he that hath a purse let him take it, and likewise a wallet, etc.

The same contrast between Jesus' lifetime and the period of the church is more abundant in the gospel of John. That writing skilfully places much of this interest of its own time in a long prophetic farewell, while still later writers deferred such post-mortem considerations actually to the period between the resurrection and the ascension which they prolonged for this purpose.

Although John most distinctly notes that the Holy Spirit belongs to a time subsequent to Jesus' lifetime, the same inference is clear in Luke's record of Jesus'

CHAP. I  *Anachronism in Thinking about Jesus*

farewell and of the day of Pentecost. It is nowhere promised to the disciples in the gospels as an immediate possession, "for the Spirit was not yet given." To this extent the evangelists did not modernize the gospel period. In another respect they may have done so in representing Jesus as filled with the Spirit. This is particularly evident in Luke, but all the gospels indicate that Jesus was baptized with water and at that event the Spirit came upon him. This was regarded as the normal experience of Christians, and was possibly transferred from the Christian experience to Jesus rather than *vice versa*. His words in Matthew, "It becometh us to fulfil all righteousness," may represent the evangelist's own consciousness that the whole story of Jesus' baptism was here receiving some color from the later church. At any rate, like another early Christian, the evangelists were prone to feel that "it behooved him in all things to be made like unto his brethren." [12]

The sufferings of Jesus were in that other author's mind when he so wrote and the passion stories of Jesus in the gospels have not been uninfluenced by experiences of his followers. How far that influence has gone we cannot now say. Other facts, including, of course, mere historical record, entered into the stories of the trial and death of Jesus. Perhaps they were written partly as example of what Christian martyrdoms should

## The Peril of Modernizing Jesus

be, but the reverse is also to be considered probable.[13] The experience of Jesus may well have been assimilated to contemporary persecutions. The evangelist who brings Jesus for trial before Herod Antipas is the very one who tells of Peter arrested by Herod Agrippa I and of Paul's hearing before Herod Agrippa II. The author of Luke and Acts is evidently aware of other parallels between the scenes of Jesus' passion and the incidents of later Christian history. Even if some later hand than his has added Jesus' forgiveness of his executioners, this too may have come from the behavior of Stephen or of later Christian martyrs.[14]

In suggesting that the details of Jesus' life are influenced by primitive Christian "modernization" one need not assume that they are wholly invented. Some may be. Modernization is often possible merely by selecting. Perhaps the length of detail alone, in the passion story, betrays the influence of contemporary theological interest. The same may be said of the abundance of predictive material in the words of Jesus, of which we have spoken. In like manner one can see how at certain stages of Christian history the Jewish criticism of Jesus' practices, or rather—which is even more suitable to our thesis—the Jewish criticism of his followers, would interest Mark's readers.[15] The relation of Jesus' career to the scriptures is more than once spoken of as an *ex post facto* discovery. Matthew's emphasis upon

CHAP. I  *Anachronism in Thinking about Jesus*

fulfilment would meet the interest of a circle of inquirers or of critics who found evidential value in coincidences of this sort and like the Bereans searched the scriptures to see whether they were there. The story when retold by Matthew and Justin Martyr naturally contained new examples and more of them, and the Fourth Gospel regarded the fulfilment of scripture as a factor determining, sometimes even consciously, the action of Jesus.

If our gospels show us, by what they contain, the selection of details to meet the early Christians' interests, their omissions, if we could discover them, would be even more illuminating. How much of Jesus' life was unwritten we are reminded by a colophon to the Fourth Gospel. The reason a detail or an event was forgotten or omitted or suppressed is not mere accident. It did not meet any interest of the author's own time or circle. In ways that we today can scarcely conjecture, the portrait of Jesus would be affected by these selections and omissions. In a few cases we can watch the later evangelists omitting from their sources details or whole passages, just as in modern biographies one can still see how the authors select material that seems to them especially interesting to our time. The kind of evidence that we have, however, may give but an imperfect idea of the extent of omission and special emphasis.

## The Peril of Modernizing Jesus — CHAP. I

So far nothing has been said of those changes in the growth of tradition which might be expected to have been the first for mention, viz., the increase of the miraculous element and the growing definiteness of Jesus' Messiahship. No doubt changes were made in these directions, but they may belong to the earliest contemporary thought about Jesus. The extent to which Messiahship was attributed to him in his lifetime by himself and by others is a most difficult problem. Changes in this matter would certainly be important, but since here illustration rather than completeness is aimed at in indicating the process of modernization in the gospels, we need not now enter the controversial field. Besides, there is a probability that in our earliest gospel Mark has exaggerated not Jesus' claim to Messiahship but his reticence about such a claim.

As to the miraculous, one can hardly doubt that time and tradition would heighten this element in the story of Jesus. Later gospels plainly move in this direction, and the evidence is familiar to all students of synoptic parallels. As with Messiahship, there is a counter tendency discoverable in which Jesus discounts the evidential value of miracle, and we ourselves may be modernizing Jesus in rejecting the miracle as gospel accretion. As is urged later, the miraculous outlook would be natural for Jesus himself and for his contemporaries, and supernatural traits would not need

CHAP. I   *Anachronism in Thinking about Jesus*

to wait long to find place in the opinion about him. Later Christians also felt that a power to work wonders was a part of Jesus' revelation to the world, as they felt that his Messiahship could not have been a secret in his lifetime. In lesser details rather than in these general directions, their viewpoint would modify the traditions that came down to them. The earlier Christian versions of Jesus were probably no less miraculous or Messianic than the one which our evangelists present us.

Far more important, however, than the restraint of the evangelists with respect to altering the surviving historical materials is the service they performed in preventing unbridled subsequent modernization, once the church accepted their writings to preserve and read, if not always inwardly digest. Merely by putting into writing an enduring, though perhaps not quite primitive, record of the life of Jesus they have limited, even if they could not entirely hinder, the free use of the imagination or the ever-shifting colors of purely oral tradition in transmitting the data of gospel history. They have served as a constant challenge and corrective to the altogether too lifelike portraits of Jesus which turn out to be posed from the artist's own mirror. Could we ever be induced to return to the portrait of Jesus as simply given by the gospels, while we might not assure ourselves that even this was entirely authentic, we should at least appreciate how much less authentic modern portraits often are. For as has already been suggested, the difference between the gospels and the real Jesus is not of a sort to lead us towards our modern preferences about him. An imagination that can clearly understand what Jesus seemed like to Mark or Luke can never be quite persuaded by the most alluring and up-to-date "recoveries of the real Jesus." As the gospels illustrate the process of modernization at work in the earliest stages, so also they supply the best materials for correcting their more recent successors.

The later modernizers, we would repeat, stand most in need of correction. Even in the other and more familiar exercise just discussed of correcting the gospel writers, the same modern preferences are often vitiating factors. Though engaged in what seems a bit of purely historical research, dealing with the distant past—the differentiation between original and later elements in the gospels, between Jesus and the evangelists—men are too prone to operate unconsciously by modern presuppositions. Thus the apocalyptic element in the gospels has been frequently laid almost exclusively to the account of the evangelists, not because there is any real evidence that Jesus also did not share it, but mainly because it is uncongenial to the present day critic. In the same way, as has been already indicated, the miraculous element is attributed to the accretion of later tradition, because the modern mind regards miracles as unhistorical, as though the tradition was ever unmiraculous! In brief, the contrast in scholarly analysis of gospel material, between what is postulated as the original and the secondary, often corresponds with suspicious accuracy to the contrast between modern preferences and modern aversions. Sometimes not the earlier but the later material in the gospels is demonstrably the less apocalyptic, the less miraculous, the more historically minded, the more psychologically reflective—in fact, the more congenial to ourselves. Whatever the reasons may be, the development of evangelic tradition was not a continuous one-way stream deviating more and more away from our modernist picture.[16]

Chapter II

# THE CAUSE AND CURE OF MODERNIZATION

THE tendency to modernize Jesus is not difficult to account for. It is natural and often unconscious. Writers and teachers about him have the same reasons as have the painters to attempt to interpret him in terms that will seem real, that is, modern and congenial to the modern mind. Few of them trouble themselves to acquire an intimate knowledge of the thinking categories of the ancient world, and until recent times, with the development of historical science and the study of contemporary materials, an attempt to place Jesus in his own setting would be neither thought of nor, if thought of, feasible.

Anachronism in thinking about Jesus has been largely due to an excusable ignorance. The gospels do not give us all the information we need, especially for the inner life of Jesus. The earliest gospels are singularly objective in their presentation of his life, so that when psychological biography becomes the style, not

CHAP. II *The Cause and Cure of Modernization*
only in novels but even in our thought of historical persons, great gaps are left to be filled by inference and conjecture if we would know the mind of Christ. These lacunae are naturally filled by modern persons with modern content. They infer what Jesus would have thought and felt from what we should think and feel. No other analogy occurs to them as needed, or as available. They do not notice that, to use the gospel metaphor, they are stitching a new patch on an old garment.

The curiosity and interest which give rise to this treatment of Jesus are not unnatural about any ancient personage. In his case there are special reasons due to his position in religion. If he is regarded as divine, while we admit that his thoughts are not like our thoughts, we have no other than human psychology to judge him by. The supreme deity is always anthropomorphized. Anthropomorphism involves not merely assigning to the deity human form. That is recognized and often resisted. It involves assigning to deity like thoughts and passions with ourselves. If anthropopathy is almost inescapable in thinking of the god or gods of purely divine nature, it is much more certain to take place with Jesus, whose human nature and earthly career seem to require it.

There have, of course, been persons and groups who have minimized the human element in Jesus. They have resolutely set themselves not "to know Christ after the flesh." Metaphysical speculation and controversy about him such as resulted in the creeds largely succeeded in dehumanizing Jesus. Already for Paul his human personality is unimportant except in certain directions. In the gospel of John with all its lifelike humanity he moves and speaks like the poet's "conscious god," self-consciously. In such circles the charge of modernizing Jesus can scarcely be brought, simply because he is not felt to be human at all. An upbringing in such an environment must have been the reason why a student, when asked of a certain narrative in the gospels what Jesus probably had in mind, replied simply that Jesus had no mind. The meaning of this startling reply to an innocent question was probably something like this. Since Jesus was very God his human life was not a series of acts and words humanly originated through the ordinary processes of mind. God need not think or consider or infer or intend or propose, and to assign such human processes to Jesus was erroneous, perhaps blasphemous. So far are God's thoughts from our thoughts.

With such thoroughgoing deification, Jesus is not identified with ourselves and modernization does not take place. But in the reaction from the purely theological Jesus which modern study of the life of Christ has brought about, the modernization of Jesus has

CHAP. II *The Cause and Cure of Modernization*

been abundant. A psychology of God, if that is what Jesus was, is not available, but in so far as he was man, he has been studied as a man and it is here that the distinction between the ancient and modern habits of mind must be observed. Liberal theology with its liberal portrait of Jesus has reveled in the emancipation of his figure from superhuman perversion. It has rightly claimed for him the reality of a personal historical existence, but in this recovery of his humanity the glaring defects of a dehumanizing theology naturally made the liberal mind less careful about its own methodological errors. In aiming to make him real and human it unconsciously made him real and modern. Complete modernization was, of course, impossible. The gospels now as ever have kept something of the ancient historical nexus between Jesus and his times. But where the evidence has been ambiguous or lacking, and sometimes almost in the face of clear evidence to the contrary, a modernized Jesus has been substituted for what was often intended to be an historical Christ. In this way the eager escape from a dehumanized Christ has been responsible for too little fidelity to the genuine first century elements which a truly historical portrait requires.

The overlooking of the errors of modernization is rendered the more easy by a common feeling that human nature has always been much the same. There is much confirmation of this feeling even when one conscientiously attempts to study and differentiate the ancient mind. Perhaps the likenesses of the ancient world appeal to us. We seem to see for example in the Old Testament and in other ancient records the very same situations as we know in modern times. The psalmists, the prophets, and others who reveal their inner lives often sound what we like to call "a very modern note." We are astonished at the identities, and probably we attend to them more easily, so that we fail to appreciate the differences. The utter confidence in God which we find in the Psalms is so similar to our own piety that we extend it like our own to a life after death, though such a life is often explicitly denied and never really asserted in the whole psalter. The insistence on social justice by the prophets is easily accepted as akin to our humanitarian and democratic ideals, and their predictions of international war are treated as though they were political weather prophets writing like skilful foreign correspondents for the Jerusalem newspapers. Even the best of scholars often forget that the earliest prophets were never writing at all. It requires real skill and a disciplined historical imagination to appreciate the fundamental difference which exists between situations ancient and modern in which individuals apparently act and think alike. Comments that are similar in general purport

CHAP. II  *The Cause and Cure of Modernization*

grow out of quite different mentality in different times, and it is easy to ignore the unexpressed difference. The very words of the Old Testament have a different meaning in their time. Its "holy" is often merely physical taboo, and so is its word "unclean." Its dietary laws were probably never even unconsciously due to sanitary reasons, and its objection to adultery belongs in the category of property rights. Even spirit is in it more material than with us. The heart is the seat of thought, not feeling, in the Bible, while the soul is frequently the physical life or nothing more than the reflexive pronoun.

These facts are generally known by scholars and so are the corresponding phenomena in the New Testament. But their lesson is often forgotten in the natural tendency to find the modern or universal in the ancient and particular.

In the case of Jesus a universality of character seems proved by subsequent history. A Galilean Jew of the first century who has become the object of devotion of so many persons of all lands, races and times would seem to have been particularly free from the limitations of age or race. If he was more than a Galilean Jew of the first century—in any sense whether human or divine—it seems to become *a priori* probable that the fullness of humanity as much as of godhead was summed up in him.

*The Peril of Modernizing Jesus*     CHAP. II

But was such unusual universality, such permanent timelessness, really there in the historical Jesus? Was his appeal to his first followers and his offense to his first foes to be found in any special aloofness from the conditions of his time? Was he not a child of his own environment like most men, both great and small? And is it not precisely the process of unhistorical modernization beginning, as we know it did, immediately after his death, that is largely responsible for the feeling of kinship or contemporaneousness which successive generations have felt for him?[1] In that case *his* permanent timelessness is merely a euphemism for *our* perpetual anachronism.

These questions must not be hastily answered either in the affirmative or in the negative. One wonders further whether with the deification of Jesus men have not somehow taken up the ancient and unmodern elements unmistakably present in the gospels into the divine aspect of his personality, so as to infer that in so far as he is like us today he is human, in so far as he is unlike us today he is divine. This would have been a curious development, but one not altogether improbable in an uncritical attitude to Jesus. We recall, for example, how the very Greek dialect of the New Testament was at one time regarded by serious philologists as the language of the Holy Ghost, because when its grammar was examined no ordinary

CHAP. II *The Cause and Cure of Modernization*

writings in the same idiom were known to exist. Jesus' parabolic teaching was long thought to be unique and hence a mark of somewhat superhuman ingenuity. Of course, now, through fuller information we know that the language of the gospels approximates the ordinary Greek of the age, and that a parabolic method, in form at least identical with the gospel examples, was precisely the method of contemporary rabbis. But the confusion of archaic and unique doubtless continues in all our popular Biblical thinking, and the quaint or unfamiliar, even the quaintness of a revered English version, easily becomes a mark of sanctity. So the hyphenated definition of Jesus' personality as both man and God, which so long in more or less distinct terms has been the background of Christian thought, has made it possible to accept the modern or universal in the gospels as human, and to assign what was unmodern and temporary not to ancient historical conditioning but to the Divine.

The modernization of Jesus is due, as we have already said, to lack of interest or trained imagination necessary to reconstruct an ancient scene. Every historian knows how great effort is required to orient oneself in an ancient age, how continuing study of contemporary materials more and more discloses the nuances and motifs of past scenes which are too subtle to be caught by the more superficial student. Even the historical novelist, who perhaps more than the historian, aims at imaginative reconstruction of the past, rarely escapes making some kind of anachronistic error. But the general thought about Jesus has not been produced by trained historians. Theologians and apologists have been the official interpreters, and their interests have not been primarily historical accuracy. We do not accuse them of wilful perversion of truth when we say that their aims have made perversion inevitable if unconscious. To prefer abstract ideas to historical fact, to use history in order to defend a religious movement, or even, as with the preacher, in order to edify the believer or to illustrate modern situations and opinions—these purposes are not compatible with single-minded historical reconstruction.

But today our thought of Jesus is not dependent so much as in the past on apologist, theologian and preacher. He is the concern of laymen, sociologists, historians, novelists, scientists. The ordinary educated man has the gospels in his hands and he feels himself qualified to make his own portrait of their central figure. No doubt these exponents have set us free from much that was perverted in the older schools of thought, but they are subject to other biases. In part they, no less than the older apologists, wish to recommend him to their own age, in part they read into him their own thoughts and standards. The alienness

CHAP. II  *The Cause and Cure of Modernization*

of Jesus is neither a subject they would emphasize, nor a feeling that they wish to cultivate. They are more quick to see likenesses than differences, and where the motive of Jesus is only to be conjectured or the fundamental principle is unexpressed they unconsciously read into his mind according to their own ways of thinking.

The unconscious process behind our claiming Jesus as one of ourselves is easily understood. There is usually even in the most emancipated minds a feeling that Jesus was probably right. In few circles would a proposal be damaged if shown to be in accordance with the mind of Christ. Everyone likes to find his own sentiment independently and unexpectedly sponsored by others. The agreement guarantees, if guarantee is necessary, the correctness of one's own opinion. One always especially endorses those parts of an address or an article of which he can say, "It is very good, I have always felt just the same way about the matter myself."

Now the gospels are books with varied content and permit of even more varied construction. Without effort, without dishonesty, and even without realizing what is happening, one can read into them and out of them one's own ideas. In fact such a process is almost unavoidable if one has any respect for the person of Jesus. We so easily assume that our own approach is the right one, and therefore that a person of Jesus' insight must have shared it. Whether we assign to him omniscience, or only a more human degree of perception, we tend to think of that knowledge of his as coinciding with what we ourselves apprehend to be true.

There is something strangely naïve in this widespread appreciation for Jesus. For, aside from its genuine recognition of his real worth, it contains so often a quite unintentional self-flattery. Nearly every word of enthusiastic praise for truths we think we find in him is really only a claim of his support for our own viewpoint. When we say that in spite of apparently unmodern, unethical, unscientific, or impractical elements in Jesus' teaching, he must have meant such and such modern, ethical, scientific or practical truths we are calmly assuming that knowledge is with us, and that in so far as he was right he must agree with our standards. And if thereupon we can argue that he does agree with our standards then we can claim—ostensibly to his honor, but really to our own—that Jesus saw ahead of his time and has been gloriously vindicated by modern experience and knowledge.[2]

The real relation between Jesus and modern standards is not to be drawn by such easy methods. The bearing of his actual historical viewpoint on the questions we ask in a very different setting must be patiently determined by more complicated methods. In-

CHAP. II  *The Cause and Cure of Modernization*

tuitional understanding and spiritual sympathy do not guarantee for the modern Christian a secure grasp upon the "mind of Christ" in any real historical sense.

This is not the place to apply or even to describe the alternative method, to indicate how without haste to secure immediate application, without short cuts to the edifying results, the study of Jesus must first be made in his own setting before he can be used for our own.[3] It is worth while to consider the kind of argument or rather of unexpressed feeling that meets any effort to present Jesus in terms that do not appeal to the hearer. The objection may be expressed somewhat bluntly thus: "But if Jesus was like that, how do you account for Christianity?"

This appeal from Christianity to Christ is a familiar feature of ecclesiastical apologetic. One recalls how the early martyrs' fidelity was used as an argument for the historicity of the miracles in the gospels. In its present form the fallacy lies in the assumption that the Christian movement could have been given its great impetus only by such qualities in its founder as would give impetus to a movement today. When analyzed the fallacy is apparent. Early Christianity was no more modern than Jesus was, and a modernized Jesus would by no means help to account for the ancient church. To be sure, recourse will doubtless be had again to the argument of universality. Many will claim that unless there

## *The Peril of Modernizing Jesus*    CHAP. II

was in Jesus a universally valid appeal his followers would never have perpetuated his memory, and efforts are made to define the nature of his influence which range all the way from mere human magnetism to the august assurance of the incarnate Son of God.

Now the ultimate success of early Christianity in winning a wide and devoted adherence rests not exclusively on the life and teaching of Jesus. How far success was due to this influence, personally, directly and accurately transmitted to the first and succeeding generations of his followers, and how far to a religious propaganda in which there was an idealized Jesus who was the future Messiah, or the present Lord, or the actual deity of an attractive cult, we find it at this late day extremely difficult to tell. In such circumstances the proverb is usually cited, that there can be no smoke without some fire. But the ratio of smoke and fire varies enormously and the smoke often is misleading as to the exact location of the fire. I am not disposed to join those who deny entirely the historicity of Jesus, but one must be prepared to admit that the religion which became the Christianity of the Roman Empire may have had but slight relation to the historical actuality of its founder. In any case the things preached about Jesus which, whether historically accurate or not, appealed to the mentality of the ancient world (like the guarantee of immortality, or protection from

CHAP. II  *The Cause and Cure of Modernization*

the power of demons) are not the things which we moderns find so significant in our restoration of him (like moral originality, or perfect spiritual or mystical harmony with God). It is instructive in this connection to contrast Harnack's careful historical summary in his *Mission of Christianity* of what appealed in Christianity's first dissemination with the same author's (I think much less historical) portrait of Jesus which he offers the modern world in his popular book *What is Christianity?*[4] Even if we should regard Jesus as entirely freed from the limitations of his environment, we can hardly extend the miracle to the whole medley which constituted his early followers. They were not moderns and if Jesus was modern it would have been in spite of, not because of, his modernness that they believed in him.

In speaking thus of the modernizing of Jesus, I have spoken rather generally. Concrete illustrations will be found, I hope, sufficiently in the subsequent chapters to illustrate what I mean. I have not intended to condemn those of us who are guilty—and who is not?—by standards which the guilty had no reason to think of, or responsibility to observe. The tendency is natural and inevitable. One may take as symbolic the ancient story of the mocking of Jesus as told in Matthew's gospel when "the soldiers of Pilate took Jesus into the prætorium and stripped him and put on him a scarlet military cloak ... and mocked him ... and when they had mocked him they took the cloak off him and put on him his own raiment."[5] The soldiers put on Jesus their own kind of clothes and we all tend to clothe him with our own thoughts.

In a self-conscious or self-critical age like ours unbridled modernization of Jesus is neither honorable nor profitable. Historical science—for better or for worse—is here with us and religion must conform to its demands in areas where religion itself claims historical foundation or validation. That history has its proper limits in religious thinking is true, but that does not justify the unhistorical modernization of Jesus in the name of either science or religion.

The tendency to modernize Jesus is not a new phenomenon in Christianity. It has always existed. The history of the study of the life of Christ, such as Schweitzer made for the last century and a half, is largely a study of this reading into Jesus the thought patterns of the age or group. In our own time different groups tend to make him in their own different images. If we were able to predict the mental atmosphere of a future generation we should be able to predict as clearly their understanding of Jesus.

The tendency is inevitable, and probably not entirely curable. To attempt to offset it is surely a reasonable

CHAP. II  *The Cause and Cure of Modernization*

ambition. The means for doing so are fairly obvious. First, the realization of our own prejudices and presuppositions. We may try to look at ourselves objectively, to realize that we, like other generations or other groups, take our own mentality for granted and quietly read it into alien figures of the past, largely because we do not make the mental exertion of trying to understand them as they were. In the case of Jesus we are anxious (often quite unconsciously and without any formal Christian acceptance of him) to secure his authority for our own point of view. We flatter ourselves by praising his universality, his modernness, his insight, since we mean by these things merely our own judgment in the areas where we are quoting him. The first necessity is to know ourselves, to allow for this tendency and to discount it and to attempt to neutralize it. These pages are intended to contribute a little to this auto-psychoanalysis.

A second method of attempting to rectify our thought of Jesus is the effort to learn the mentality of his environment. There is much to be said for a knowledge of Moslem or oriental mentality as a corrective, though I suspect that the claims of orientalists to understand Jesus more truly are often overdone, as indeed are the claims of all specialists. I recall for example the characteristic behavior of three specialists who, meeting at my home one evening, happened (perhaps at my instigation) to fall into a conversation on the historical character of Jesus. One was the late Professor G. F. Moore, who naturally emphasized Jesus' likeness to the Jewish rabbis; one was Professor F. G. Peabody, who stressed the practical ethical aspects of Jesus' character; the third was Professor Otto of Marburg, an expert in Western and oriental mysticism, for whom Jesus was very much of an old Jewish holy man. Nevertheless, within limits, a specialized knowledge of Semitic antiquity in general and of late Judaism in particular is quite valuable. Beyond that a feeling and an imagination for the ancient world, whether Semitic or Aryan, is a most useful corrective.

The third and most tangible corrective is the gospel records. They are a standing enemy as well as a standing ally to the modernization of Jesus. Their assistance to the movement consists in their own multiform suggestion, which allows us to find by selection, somewhere within their varied contents, proof-text support for almost any reconstruction of Jesus that we desire. They also leave so many gaps to be filled, so much outward material for our own psychological interpretation that, without actively suggesting each new portraiture of the master, they coöperate with any nuclear prejudice we may have by giving us pliable historical material for our purpose. How such simple biographies can be so variously understood is truly remark-

CHAP. II  *The Cause and Cure of Modernization*

able. It would seem incredible if we did not know sane people who have held such varying views. But a knowledge of present day human nature and a new appreciation of the endless ambiguity and non-committal quality of the records will enable one to see how easily such opposite conclusions can be drawn.

But even more the gospels recall us to the Jesus of history. One shudders to think what would have happened to him in successive generations of oral tradition and Christian idealization if tradition and idealization had not been held in check by such written records. Some measure of what might have taken place we can sometimes draw from other purely oral religions and traditions. In Christianity itself before the gospel story was written and wherever it has been ignored, invention and imagination have had a free course. By putting down in writing this material the evangelists set a bound to change. Still today, as in the past, every imaginative portrait of Jesus must somehow square itself with these persistent standards.[6]

Many might suppose that in a book like this which aims at recovering the historical Jesus much attention would be given to an evaluation of the gospel evidence, both in general and in detail. This is a familiar exercise to New Testament scholars which I do not intend to indulge in. I can avoid it partly because I can say in a general way that I accept the findings of modern criticism. I shall be especially cautious about using the Fourth Gospel as history at all and I shall assume that the other three, and the oral tradition which preceded them, have been already affected by the interests of the early church; that is, as I have illustrated in the previous chapter, they have already been modernized. To distinguish in these books the historical and the unhistorical is a delicate task. Here there is more agreement in principle among scholars than there is in application. Subjective criteria are too easily accepted, and an item which is suspected by one scholar has for another the authentic marks of historicity. It has often happened that the stone which the critics rejected has become for a new school of critics the head of the corner. Nearly every idealization of Jesus makes of the evangelists its convenient scapegoat and each critic regards Jesus, i.e., his own particular Jesus, as, in the phrase of Matthew Arnold, "far above the heads of his reporters."

But I the more gladly avoid the sifting of gospel evidence since that would put the emphasis in quite the wrong place. I agree that for historical study the scrutinizing of the gospel material is essential, and I am prepared to engage in it at another time; but now I would direct attention to the defects in our own makeup. When I read a life of Christ that in the most careful approved fashion describes at length the un-

CHAP. II  *The Cause and Cure of Modernization*

historical character of the gospels and the aspects of their viewpoint which are to be rejected as late and secondary, but then proceeds to construct a portrait of the Master shot through with modern standards of value, I feel like saying, "Why beholdest thou the mote that is in thy brother's eye, but considerest not the beam that is in thine own eye?" In other words, a principal obstacle to the accurate recovery of Jesus is not so much the untrustworthiness of the evangelists, as the prejudices and presuppositions of our own minds, what the psychologist used to call "the apperceptive mass." To recognize the defect in the evangelists, and even in others of our own age with whose conclusions we do not agree, is easy. What we need is —if I may correct the poet slightly—to see ourselves as we see others.

In comparing ourselves with the evangelists we often note how loosely they and, indeed, all the New Testament writers quote the Old Testament. Short passages are taken completely out of their context and given a force which has only the slightest verbal likeness to the matter in hand. We almost laugh at the naïveté of the early Christians. They seem never to have tried to recover the actual historical context of the passages they are reading or quoting. Had they done so they would scarcely have found their quotations relevant or apposite. But this well known defect of Old Testament citation in the New is quite analogous to our own treatment of the latter. The twentieth century is often more meticulous than the first in its respect for the literary and historical context of the Bible that it quotes; our shortcoming is more often to ignore what I think we may call the "psychological context" of scripture.

In thus girding at modernists I do not wish to be understood as urging a return to the theological Jesus of earlier and less critical schools. Still less do I want to claim that I am immune from other temptations.

In particular, the aim of this book is to minimize the modernness of Jesus. Yet it would be an error to write down as exclusively genuine everything archaic, obsolete, alien, uncongenial, grotesque or difficult for us in the gospels or in their interpretation. I suppose that is the risk in our present approach. The reverse of modernization tends to over-archaize him.

Probably the real difficulty on each side is the unwillingness to leave Jesus unknown and unexplained. The gaps in our knowledge of him are many. Both Jesus and his reporters are often silent just when we should like to know. Some of the most significant questions about him, not only external details like the year of his birth and of his death, but inward questions like his real attitude to Messiahship, are left to us unsolved problems. Let us recall the words of the inscrutable Jesus himself, "No one knows the Son, save the Father." He promises no further exception.

Chapter III

# THE JEWISHNESS OF THE GOSPELS

PROBABLY the best way to remind ourselves of the unmodernness of Jesus' mind is to show his likeness to the thinking of his environment. That environment is not only an archaic one, marked by the absence of many modern ways of thought; it is a quite distinctive one within the ancient world. For the Jewish people to whom Jesus belonged and whose mentality he shared had even among the ancients and perhaps even among the Semites their own peculiar development. The contrast in thought between Jesus and ourselves is, therefore, not merely between ancient and modern, but also between oriental and western and to a slight extent between Jew and Gentile. Of course, our modern western Gentile mind has known and inherited, especially through the Bible, much of this alien viewpoint. The difference between Jesus and ourselves is not so much what he had that we now lack, but what we have added in methods of thought, assumptions and presuppositions. Our modern plus often overshadows and even cancels the ancient though still familiar Jewish viewpoint. This situation explains why so much in these pages is concerned with the reiterated denial to Jesus of concepts which we hold.

In comparing the Jesus of the synoptic gospels with the Jewish mind of his time and place we are fortunately situated. To most of us the mental antecedents and background of Homer, of Omar Khayyam, and even of the authors of Job or of the Fourth Gospel are obscure, if not altogether unknowable. But first century Palestinian Judaism is either directly known pretty well or else may be safely conjectured from its pre-Christian antecedents or its Tannaitic successors. We do not know all we should like to know about it. The great variety within the Judaism of that day makes it difficult to classify all strands of religious belief from the writers of the apocalypses to the new covenanters of Damascus. Our relatively recent acquaintance with these two varieties of Jewish thought reminds us of the wide scope for diversity even within the circle of loyal Judaism. Fortunately our present object is not to compare Jesus' views with those of special sets among his contemporaries, but to consider rather his general horizons and assumptions, the methods of thought, the furniture of the mind. For this our knowledge of contemporary Judaism is adequate, and we believe the evidence confirms what should be obvious

CHAP. III  *The Jewishness of the Gospels*

*a priori,* without need of argument, that in these respects Jesus was a child of his time and place.

There is one aspect of this correspondence which is notable enough to deserve prior mention. It is the relative absence of the Hellenic element in the synoptic gospels. Coming to us now in Greek, from an age when under Paul and other teachers from the Diaspora Christianity had already made some adjustments to Greek ways of thinking, the synoptic gospels still breathe the atmosphere of Palestine in thought and language. This unhellenic character will be denied by some who believe that the birth stories are affected by Gentile myths or the sayings of Jesus influenced by the gnostic or esoteric teaching of the cults. Others will explain it as due to the early date of certain Aramaic sources, out of which the Greek is literally and slavishly rendered. I cannot here enter into these controversies, but I may express my conviction that the gospels have preserved accurately much of the genuine Jewish character of the gospel story—Palestinian in setting, of course, but also in the matter and manner of the discourse and dialogue.

What a less faithful or less Jewish tradition would have done is well illustrated by the Fourth and later gospels or even by such a single conflate saying as the Oxyrhynchus logion: "Jesus saith, The kingdom of God is within you [the Gospel of Luke] and Know your-

*The Peril of Modernizing Jesus*

selves [the Delphic γνῶθι σαυτόν]." The moment Christianity met pure heathenism its first demand was to "turn from idols and to serve the living and true God." But I can find no evidence that for the first readers or writers of the gospels this missionary problem was present. There is no polemic against polytheism or idolatry. One would never know from the synoptic gospels that there were any Gentile cities and large permanent Gentile settlements in Palestine.

Indeed, it is possible to raise the question, though this is rarely done, whether the gospels do not disclose sometimes the accession of Jewish coloring rather than its diminution. The Gospel of Matthew in particular, so far from representing a stage removed from the primitive Jewishness and approaching towards a Gentile Christianity, may be suspected of Jewish Christian reimpregnation both in thought and in language. We can compare it with at least one of its sources and must often, both here and elsewhere, allow for the possibility that the Christian tradition in some areas and in some groups added Jewish traits to the original Jewish story of Jesus. Perhaps teachings and sayings of other rabbis have by Christians been assigned to their own teacher. Matthew practices the Jewish avoidance of the divine name by saying "Kingdom of Heaven" instead of "Kingdom of God." Matthew calls Gentiles "swine," and Jerusalem "the holy city," and explicitly

CHAP. III  *The Jewishness of the Gospels*

denies the suggestion that Jesus would destroy the law or that his followers were to preach to Gentiles or Samaritans. There are, of course, traits in Matthew that look the other way, but these suggestions may provide a counter hypothesis to the method of Bultmann, who in his history of the synoptic tradition assigns so much change to the Hellenic phase of the gospel.

The Jewish mentality of the gospels, whether due to tradition or to Jesus himself, is well indicated by their language. Language indeed is not the same as thought, and thoughts of an alien culture can be expressed in almost any language. Yet to a certain extent language is determinative of thought. What we cannot say is hard to think, and what we can say often determines our thinking. All early Semitic thought has been affected by the fact that this family of languages is poor in abstract terms, that its psychology is expressed by terms of physiological localization, and that its conjunctions tend to be coördinating rather than subordinating. Hence the sheer vocabulary and style of the gospels are reminders to us of Jesus' own non-modern mind. Not always do we recognize the archaic quality of the terms.

Take for example the saying of the single eye:

The lamp of the body is the eye; if therefore thine eye be single, thy whole body shall be full of light. But if thine eye be evil, thy whole body shall be full of darkness.

At best this carries a metaphor too far, but the original meaning of the metaphor is lost to most modern readers. Only when we know that in Jewish speech "evil eye" means a grudging, miserly character, while "singleness" is the exact word for its opposite, viz., generosity, can we recognize that in this passage Jesus is not talking at all of singleness of purpose or simplicity of character, but, as often elsewhere, of generosity in our gifts. The idiom in the original with "eye" has made possible by extension of metaphor the reference to the whole body as light or dark, which in our language is untranslatable because we have not the same physical term for stinginess. Perhaps our word is "close-fisted" and to reproduce in our terms the thought of Jesus we should have to alter the whole parable: The door to the body is the hand; he whose charity is open-handed . . . but when the hand is closed, etc.

Other phrases, like this one, are so familiar to us from reading the New Testament that their relation to first century Judaism is not always obvious to us. Specially interesting are those phrases of Jesus which while absent from the Old Testament are nevertheless to be found in the rabbis. One of these is "to taste of death," found in all the gospels. Another is the combination "flesh and blood." Mammon (wealth) is also a contemporary word. It is not found in the Old Testament but appears soon thereafter in Hebrew in

CHAP. III     *The Jewishness of the Gospels*

the text of Ecclesiasticus, in the Damascus writing and in *Pirḳe Aboth:*

R. Jose used to say "the mammon of thy neighbor shall be dear to thee as thine own" or "the salt of mammon is almsgiving."

The word is particularly common in the Aramaic Targums where of course it obviously replaces Hebrew words. Frequently there we find it followed by דשקר which seems to indicate that Luke's "mammon of unrighteousness" was a fixed combination like the modern cliché "filthy lucre" which comes from Tyndale's New Testament, or like the seventeenth century English phrase "lucre of gain."

Mention was made of the Jewish substitute for the divine name in Matthew's "Kingdom of Heaven." The other gospels bear witness probably to similar contemporary circumlocution on Jesus' own part. In the dialogue in Mark between the high priest and Jesus, the former inquires, "Art thou the Christ, the son of the blessed?" while Jesus replies, "Ye shall see the son of man seated at the right hand of power." Both surrogates for God—"the blessed," "power"—are easily illustrated from the rabbis. The former seems to Professor Burkitt "so peculiarly Jewish that the question of the High-priest and the answer he actually got must have some foundation in fact."[1] Even Luke, the most

Gentile of the writers, is not without his Jewish background. He characteristically uses for the deity the term "most high." This is what Jews regularly employed in representing Gentiles as speaking of the Jewish god. But Luke also uses "heaven" very much as First Maccabees does in place of God: "Father, I have sinned before heaven and in thy sight," and in Luke too we apparently get that impersonal plural which the rabbis also employ in place of God: "Thou fool, this night they require thy life of thee."

No part of a language group is more distinctive or idiomatic than the picturesque phrases it uses for superlatives. We should recognize as familiar in our own time the expressions "to hunt a needle in a haystack," "to miss hitting a barndoor," "to cross your t's and dot your i's," "to be as alike as two peas," and we know that other modern languages often have just as distinctive expressions which differ entirely from our own.[2] Many of the superlatives used in the gospels can, in a most interesting way, be paralleled from the rabbinic literature.[3] For "camel through the needle's eye" the Babylonian Jews said "elephant through the needle's eye." Both express the impossible. Whether camels were known in Babylonia or not, elephants were not familiar in Palestine. But camel occurs again in the gospel as the big creature, over against the gnat: "Strain out the gnat and swallow the camel." Then

CHAP. III   *The Jewishness of the Gospels*

we have rabbinic parallels to the removal of a mote or a beam; they are spoken of in connection with censoriousness, as in the gospels. The foreign objects are, however, between the eyes, or between the teeth. From another sphere of life we have the minimum expressed by a mustard seed, the maximum by a tree or mountain. Even more typical of the bookish, letter-conscious scribe or scholar is the mention by Jesus of the immutability in the law of even the jot or the tittle. The former is the smallest letter of the alphabet; the latter is a decorative flourish placed over letters of the Old Testament texts in Hebrew frequently mentioned not by the Latin name tittle or *titulus* but by the Semitic word for horn (so the Greek in Matthew) or thorn or crown. Thus in speaking of the written text of the Hebrew law Jesus uses a term not applicable to other scripts or even to secular writings in Hebrew or Aramaic but to the contemporary scrolls of the Torah alone. It is much as if a seventeenth century reader of the Authorized Version had asserted the inspiration and immutability of its text even to the decorative woodcuts of the chapter initials.

Another characteristic of Jesus' teaching is the parable. To readers whose knowledge of literature is limited to the classics, the Bible, and modern writings, these parables appear unique. But the student of first century Judaism recognizes in them a striking con-

*The Peril of Modernizing Jesus*　　　CHAP. III

formity precisely to the style of the rabbis. One may dispute whether the gospel parables are not more polished and vivid, they may seem so because they are more familiar; they are of course less legal or scholastic, but the rabbinic parallels with their similar interrogative introduction, with their assortment of King parables and with even closer likeness in occasional details again remind us how the records of Jesus fit the literary genres of his time and place. Many have remarked that the synoptic parable in spite of one or two allegories in John 10 and 15 is really unparalleled in the Gospel of John. This difference is not so much a contrast between the literary personalities of the evangelists as a disclosure of their relative distance from or nearness to the original Jewish Jesus.[4]

When we attempt to pass from vocabulary and literary forms to the thinking processes of Jesus our task of analysis becomes more difficult, but nothing that we discover in the gospels contrasts with what we can learn of the Jewish mentality of his time. Chesterton once spoke of Jesus as making "furious use of *a fortiori* argument." There is much in the gospels to confirm this. "If ye being evil know how to give good gifts, how much more shall your heavenly Father," etc.; "If God so clothe the grass," etc.; "Is not a sparrow sold for two farthings," etc. In these and other passages Jesus certainly argues from the less to the

CHAP. III  *The Jewishness of the Gospels*

greater, from the less important to the more important. The same method, called "the heavy and the light," was employed by the rabbis.[5] The subject matter is often different. Jesus draws his inference from nature or humanity. His theological method, we must recognize, is often inference from the human to the divine. For the rabbis the method is most familiar in their use of scripture incidents or requirements. Even here we have Jesus' implication in the words "a greater than Jonah," or "a greater than Solomon is here," "a prophet, yea more than a prophet." "It shall be more tolerable for Sodom and Gomorrah in the day of judgment," etc.

Here is one rabbinic example, out of many, that illustrates not only the *a fortiori* argument but some traits of parable that we have spoken of, and the question of resurrection which will be mentioned presently:

The emperor (Hadrian) said to Rabban Gamaliel, "You say that those who sleep will come to life again; have they not turned to dust and can dust come to life?"

Then spoke Gamaliel's daughter to her father, "Let him alone, I will answer him. In our city," she said, "there are two potters; one makes (the vessels) out of water, the other out of clay. Which of them deserves the greater praise?"

The emperor answered, "He who makes out of water."

She said, "If he (God) creates a man out of water (i.e., human seed), how much more can he do it out of clay (i.e., the dust of the grave)?"[6]

A similar *a fortiori* argument for immortality is drawn from the fact that it was possible when a glass vessel made by blowing was broken, to restore it by blowing it again. "If there is restoration for that which is formed by the breath of a man, how much more for that which was formed by an inbreathing on God's part." [7]

In both the *a fortiori* argument and in the parable, reliance is placed primarily on the force of analogy. A clever use of this occurs when Jesus gets the interlocutor to express first a judgment on the illustration. Thus he sets the situation and asks a question. "Which of the two [sons] did the will of his father?" "When the owner of the vineyard comes, what will he do to those husbandmen?" "Which of them [two debtors forgiven by their creditor] will love him most?" "Which of these three [priest, Levite, Samaritan] seems to thee to have proved neighbor to him that fell among thieves?" [8]

This method of argument was used effectively by the Old Testament prophets, even to the extent of acting the parable or telling it as real, as in Nathan's parable of the ewe lamb. It is also very characteristic of the rabbis. Although Jesus' refrain, "He that hath ears to hear let him hear," expresses it somewhat differently, his whole method of getting his hearers to answer their own question is well summed up in the neat rabbinic

CHAP. III    *The Jewishness of the Gospels*

phrase: "May thy ears hear what thy mouth speaks."

Another example of the same form of argument deals like Paul with the question of the resurrection body and uses like Paul the grain of wheat. Some one asked Rabbi Meir: "I know that those who sleep will come to life again ... But when they rise will they rise naked or in their garments?" He replied, "In this matter one must apply to the grain of wheat the deduction from the lesser to the more important. If the grain of wheat, that comes naked into the soil, grows forth again with no one knows how many coverings, how much more true is it of the righteous who are buried in their clothes that they will also rise again in their garments." [9]

Even to the characteristic scribal use of scripture the gospels provide undoubted parallels. Just as Paul and the Alexandrian Christians approximate the allegory of the Alexandrian Jews, so Jesus the Palestinian is closer to the method of the Aramaic rabbis. In his citation of the Old Testament in argument, Jesus, whatever his freedom from the law in practice, behaved like a good Jew. A notable instance of method is his reply to the question about the resurrection. In citing the words from the passage called "The Bush," "I am the God of Abraham, the God of Isaac and the God of Jacob," [10] he astutely argues that since God would not call himself the God of dead men, these patriarchs

*The Peril of Modernizing Jesus*     CHAP. III

must have been alive when, years after their death, God calls himself their God. Such arguments are doubtless convincing only to those who are willing to accept them. This is precisely the form of argument, however, if not this identical example, which the rabbis used.

Numerous texts of scripture were used by the rabbis to prove the resurrection, often one from each of the three parts of the canon, but only those from the Law would be really effective against Samaritans and Sadducees, for these deniers of the resurrection did not accept the Prophets and the Writings as authoritative. Jesus also in arguing with Sadducees takes his text from the Torah. A story is told by Professor Moore of a "discussion between Rabban Gamaliel (II) and the Sadducees: The Sadducees asked Rabban Gamaliel, 'Where is the evidence that the holy one, blessed is He, brings the dead to life?' He replied, 'In the Law and in the Writings'; but they did not accept his proof. [The three passages are given and the Sadducees' objection to each.] Finally, Gamaliel quoted to them the words of Deuteronomy: the land which 'the Lord sware to your fathers to give to them.' It is not said *to you*, but *to them;* from this the resurrection of the dead is proved." [11]

The same verse of Deuteronomy figures also in a controversy with the Samaritans, who denied that the resurrection of the dead was to be found in the Law.

CHAP. III  *The Jewishness of the Gospels*

R. Eliezer ben Jose charges them with mutilating their scriptures by leaving out "to them," without gaining anything by it, for the resurrection is proved elsewhere in the Law.[12]

Among many other texts used as arguments in the same section of the Talmud is the commandment of the Law: "And thereof shall ye give the Lord's portion (Terumah) to Aaron the priest."[13] "Did Aaron live forever? Is it not true that he did not even enter the land of Israel, that they might give this portion? The words teach that he is to live in the future and the Israelites give him the portion."

In all these cases, including that of Jesus, the argument is chronological. Apparent anachronism in the scriptural expression can, it is claimed, only be avoided by assuming the doctrine of a resurrection, which makes the early patriarchs eternal contemporaries.

These parallels to Jesus' reply about the resurrection are given at length to show the rabbinic character of that reply. The passage is not really characteristic of the gospel teaching as a whole and objection may well be made to placing much stress upon it. Indeed it, and the few similar passages, like the dialogue on David's Lord and David's son, are usually apologized for by Christians as exceptional, unworthy of Jesus, and really unlike him. His teaching elsewhere seems so direct, so free from subtlety or mere dialectic.

*The Peril of Modernizing Jesus*   CHAP. III

Now this contrast between the rabbinic and synoptic material is a true one and may indeed go back to the difference in the sources. But I suspect that the different channels of transmission are even more responsible. In the Christian oral lay tradition the original words of Jesus become more direct and epigrammatic, while in the tradition of the rabbinic schools the rabbinic method loses nothing of its subtle dialectic character. The masters in each series were probably more alike than their disciples.

That the subjects of Jesus' thought were much those of his contemporaries is also evident from the records that remain. Like a Jew's his thinking was practical, ethical, and concrete rather than metaphysical and abstract. Though many of his sayings have come to us without exact setting they were doubtless due to real situations in his life, personal or public. The questions asked him are not hard to fit into the Jewish scene—about John the Baptist, about the resurrection, about tribute to Caesar. Between groups or even definite parties these were moot questions, and whether Jesus' answer coincided with one group or another makes no difference to us in realizing the thought world of his time. Even if we did not know that his summary of the law in the Golden Rule coincided with an answer of Rabbi Hillel, or his summary by the two commandments of love with a later answer of Rabbi Akiba, the fact that the question was put to him and answered

CHAP. III  *The Jewishness of the Gospels*

somehow by him indicates the contemporary contents of his mind. One can hardly think of a Jew much earlier or a Christian much later even trying to deal with that question. Sometimes we are given the occasion of his replies—certain recent disasters in Jerusalem which raise the question of the relation of personal guilt to apparently undiscriminating and accidental punishment. John's fatal criticism of Herod and Herodias led most directly to the question put to Jesus, "Is it lawful for a man to put away his wife and marry another?" The point is not that Jesus' answer coincides or conflicts with one or another contemporary answer, but that the subjects on which he spoke and thought are the subjects of contemporary thought and teaching.

How far Jesus agreed with the judgments of his time we need not now consider. Such comparisons are not easy to make—not even in the case of that central authority of contemporary Judaism, the Mosaic law. That his opinions as well as the subjects on which he expressed them were to be found here or there within the wide variety and range of Palestinian Judaism seems to me altogether probable. We can infer that on the resurrection of the dead he agreed with the Pharisees against the Sadducees but on the authority of the oral law he was more in sympathy with the latter than the former. On the treatment of criminals like the woman taken in adultery he was doubtless nearer the lenient school of Hillel than the severe school of Shammai. About divorce he may have sided more nearly with the rigorists. With regard to oaths he is quoted in words that would fit the Essenes. With respect to the coming of God's Kingdom his anticipation may have been more like John the Baptist's than that of the so-called zealots and their revolutionary forerunners.

Taking the gospels then at their face value they attest what we should have expected in advance from any early and trustworthy reports of Jesus. His speech as quoted, his categories of thought, his subjects of discussion, were all in the manner and range of contemporary Judaism. This agreement, so far from being disconcerting, should be to us rather reassuring. Had the gospels come from remoter contacts with Jesus they would have revealed different cultural qualities. A more modern or familiar or un-Jewish picture would have been thereby more suspect. As it is, an analysis of the Jewish character of the books, though we have made it with no apologetic motive, turns out to be a rather striking argument for a degree of historical probability in the ancient records. The very style rings true to first century Palestine so far as we can know that environment from other sources. In revealing the Jewishness of Jesus the gospels supply at the same time credentials for the general accuracy and contemporaneousness of their own material.

Chapter IV

# JESUS AND THE MENTALITY OF OUR AGE

IF THE evidence of Jesus' Jewishness, discussed in the previous chapter, is valid, the inference that Jesus' mind stands in radical contrast to the mentality of our age is also valid, though it will come as a surprise to some readers. The question may well be asked: Why if Jesus' thought and speech are so alien to our own has this essential Jewishness not been more fully appreciated?

One reason, no doubt, has been in the past the lack of general knowledge about his environment. Thanks to the efforts of both Jews and Christians, men like Abrahams, Montefiore, Billerbeck, Fiebig, Klausner, Herford and G. F. Moore, the Christian student today can know first century Judaism much more fully and more accurately than was possible for him a few years ago. This knowledge rather than any better information about Jesus makes us able to see how Jesus fits his setting as the hand fits the glove.

*The Peril of Modernizing Jesus*  CHAP. IV

The older Christian interpretation wished to emphasize the difference between Jesus and his contemporaries. Even the Jewish material was studied from this angle of contrast, and of course the gospels with their prevailing atmosphere of conflict gave color to the most extreme views. Impelling apologetic motives affected the Christian. He wished to maintain the religious and moral superiority of Jesus' teaching.

Still more influential, though only in recent times, has been the Christian claim of originality in Jesus. Dependence on his environment or even similarity to it came to be regarded as belittling to Jesus. He must be thought of as unique, even *in vacuo*. Whenever Jesus and the rabbis seem to say or believe the same thing it has been customary to whittle the likeness away by reading between the lines implications that would create the maximum difference. Now of course "when two men say the same thing it is not the same," as the proverb tells us, and of course Jesus differed from his contemporaries in some undefinable degree. But uniqueness whether as God or as man is a very different matter, and in the case of Jesus appears to be a modern inference from theological presuppositions or perhaps a human substitute for divine attributes, rather than a deduction from a careful comparison of the historical evidence for each body of teaching—that

CHAP. IV     *Jesus and the Mentality of Our Age*

of Jesus on the one hand and that of Judaism on the other.

Independence, originality, uniqueness—if I may use an ascending scale of terms—is sometimes assumed for Jesus on the basis of general considerations. That he was put to death out of Jewish hostility seems an unquestioned fact. That a new and revolutionary religious movement grew out of his career is another datum of history. But neither the crucifixion nor the Christian church is testimony to any extreme novelty in Jesus. How much must one differ from current opinion to be killed for the difference? Certainly not entirely—there must be a general meeting of minds or the differences are not apparent. It is those who, with so much of our own point of view, nevertheless diverge in small but vital issues that we crucify. If they did not so largely share our presuppositions and assumptions, our concepts of thinking and methods of argument, we would send them rather to the asylum than to the gallows. As Paul, the ex-Pharisee and Hebrew of the Hebrews, was hounded by Jewish hatred, so earlier it was with Jesus, the Jew. Precisely because he was a Jew—perhaps even a Pharisee and a scribe, were the scribes and Pharisees so sensitive to the slightest unorthodoxies of Jesus. Had he been a Greek, a foreigner, or even less Jewish as a Jew, they would have lacked enough rap-

*The Peril of Modernizing Jesus*        CHAP. IV

port to permit controversy or debate. And one may be sure that his opponents were more conscious of the difference than he was. Both his popularity and his unpopularity were due to Jesus' real contact with the circumstances of his environment.

Nor, on the other hand, can we argue from the rise of the Christian church to the non-Jewishness of Jesus. The church was not Jesus' own creation nor does it primarily express the differentia of Jesus from his environment. In its time it has been, like Jesus himself, continuously in accord with much of its environment, changing with that environment, whether Jewish, Hellenistic, mediæval or modern. Its success has lain precisely in this accordance and not in an initial uniqueness of its founder.

The best proof-text for the originality of Jesus is the incident in the very forefront of the oldest gospel:

> And they go into Capernaum: and straightway on the sabbath day he entered into the synagogue and taught. And they were astonished at his teaching: for he taught them as having authority, and not as the scribes. [Then follows the exorcising of the unclean spirit.] And they were all amazed, insomuch that they questioned among themselves, saying, What is this? a new teaching! with authority he commandeth even the unclean spirits, and they obey him.[1]

Here at least we seem to have a primitive witness to the newness and difference of Jesus' teaching. Much

CHAP. IV    *Jesus and the Mentality of Our Age*

speculation has been spent on the meaning of this passage in Mark. What Matthew understood by it is shown by what he used it for. He transferred it to the end of the Sermon on the Mount as a summary opinion of his compilation of Jesus' words relating to the standards of contemporary Judaism. In Mark's context the differentia of Jesus appears to be the authority with which he controls even the unclean spirits. But perhaps Mark had in mind not merely the accompaniments of his teaching—but his manner and method. If so, his further meaning escapes us. No doubt when he wrote the contrast between Jesus and the scribes had been greatly sharpened. But there is no reason to suppose that the distinctions which we should notice on each side—either the scribal dialectic of citing texts and rabbis, or Jesus' picturesque and epigrammatic utterances—were in the mind of Mark or of Jesus' hearers.

Another factor conduces to the minimizing of the Jewish element in Jesus. An ancient attitude is more obviously temporary than is a present one, and if an ancient element has been transcended at the beginning of Christian history that shows that it is "essential" or "permanent" rather than particularistic. Thus every effort is made to show how unprovincial and timeless was Jesus' preaching and how easily the content of the gospel could be transposed into the religious feeling of Hellenism. As Schweitzer says:

## The Peril of Modernizing Jesus CHAP. IV

The theological study of history is apt, even though unconsciously, to give ear to practical considerations. At bottom, it is guided by the instinct that whatever in the primitive Gospel is capable of being Hellenised may also be considered capable of being modernised. It therefore seeks to discern in Paul's teaching—as also in that of Jesus—as much as possible that "transcends Judaism," that has the character of "universal religion" and "essential Christianity." It is haunted by the apprehension that the significance of Christianity, and its adaptation to our times, is dependent on justifying the modernisation of it on the lines hitherto followed and in accordance with the historical views hitherto current.[2]

But the most effective reason why the modern student overlooks the archaism of Jesus and transposes him to our own mentality has yet to be mentioned. More influential than either ignorance or desire to establish originality is the tacit assumption that our own outlook is correct and that Jesus inevitably shared it. The modernizing here is unconscious and spontaneous. In fact another Weltanschauung than our own is rarely considered. We forget how many of our thought categories are distinctly modern. The rise of science, with its notions of cause and effect, evolution and natural law, has moulded our thinking. This is true quite as much of our study of past history as it is in natural science itself. Indeed, these modern assumptions are not dependent on our knowing in detail any science at all.

CHAP. IV  *Jesus and the Mentality of Our Age*

The ideas of impersonal law, of causation, of genetic development, or of progress come to us as part of our whole civilization, they are imbibed rather than studied, taken for granted rather than proved.

It is one of the chief services of the recent emphasis on the apocalyptic element in the gospels that it has rediscovered the contrast between Jesus' outlook on history and our own. We have found in the gospels—it would not be too strong to say, rediscovered—an expectation of future world events so catastrophic and supernatural that they jar with our own easy modern conception of slowly evolving historical processes. According to these elements in the records Jesus and his contemporaries anticipated a series of world cataclysms, the coming of the Kingdom of God with power, a definite day of judgment. These views, no matter how sketchily and tentatively they were held, were not merely figurative and spiritual descriptions of evolutionary movements in human society nor of "some far off divine event to which the whole creation moves." They were literal, and they were part of a mentality that thought in terms of epochs sharply marked off, of historical crises that were in a sense precipitated onto human and natural affairs from without. The Jewish mind conceived the future like the past as a planned but not automatic series, and no matter how little they agreed on the plan for that future, the nature of the epochs, the dating of the episodes, they agreed far more with each other than with the typical modern interpreters of history. In this unmodern perspective on history Jesus was distinctly a child of his time. Though the Jews developed very early the writing of history—centuries indeed before the Greeks—their interpretation of it was by no means modern. And the idea of progress has no more place in the Sermon on the Mount than it has in the Old Testament or Herodotus.

While the apocalyptic outlook of some of Jesus' Jewish contemporaries is now admitted and even of his first followers, the idea that he himself held the same assumptions is still widely resisted, in spite of the services of Johannes Weiss and Albert Schweitzer and many of their converts. Much is made of the disciples' misunderstanding, of the evangelists' editorial influence, and even of suggested interpolation. Variations in apocalyptic detail are treated as evidence that Jesus held no apocalyptic view at all, while the parables or the Fourth Gospel are appealed to as teaching the growth of the Kingdom of God, the gradualness of the second coming and the inwardness of the judgment. Because we do not combine moral teaching with such an outlook we suppose Jesus could not. Because the outcome in nineteen hundred years has not tallied, at least not yet, with gospel prophecies, we avoid ad-

## Jesus and the Mentality of Our Age

mitting that Jesus was mistaken by somehow denying the meaning or the authenticity of the apocalyptic words attributed to him, or by construing some other passages in a modern or spiritual sense.

All this exegetical effort, while it is partly intended to protect the infallibility of Jesus or to give him a modern consistency, is, I am convinced, more or less accepted by the great bulk of liberal scholars primarily because the apocalyptic outlook is uncongenial to the modern mind. It is difficult to make our strictly historical imagination overcome such pervasive and unconscious modern preferences.

Before the unmodern apocalyptic outlook of Jesus came to be appreciated by recent scholars, the Jewishness of his viewpoint was suggested by another controversial problem—the Higher Criticism of the Old Testament. It was evident—for example from words in the dialogue already mentioned, "David therefore called him Lord"—that Jesus assumed the Davidic authorship of the 110th Psalm and probably held the current Jewish view of authorship for all the Old Testament books. That view indeed prevailed in Christian circles and still widely prevails. But for those who accepted the findings of modern literary science, the question of Jesus' accuracy was raised, and unless escape was found by supposing that Jesus, knowing better himself, nevertheless accommodated himself to the

*The Peril of Modernizing Jesus*     CHAP. IV

theories of his hearers, it became necessary to suppose that Jesus simply and naturally accepted the current Jewish theory of Old Testament authorship.

In another area also moderns have long questioned the viewpoint apparently accepted by Jesus, viz., demoniac possession as the diagnosis of certain disorders of body or mind, and have again been willing to admit that he accepted or at least voluntarily behaved as though he accepted conceptions or theories which are rejected by the modern world. What has been recognized perforce in these two or three areas needs to be recognized in much wider fields: that Jesus shared the thought of his own age and was quite unconscious of the differing viewpoints which we today take for granted so easily, not only for ourselves but for every historical character that we admire.

A more inclusive but less observed difference of viewpoint is Jesus' unmodern theism. Not merely in the realm of future history but everywhere Jesus accepts the direct intervention of God in human affairs far more completely than even the most conservative of modern theists. We are hardly able, for example, to read the beatitudes without considering how far the traits of character or circumstances described tend themselves to produce the associated blessing. We appeal to the natural effects of wealth or poverty, of love or hatred, as somehow confirming Jesus' verdict upon

CHAP. IV   *Jesus and the Mentality of Our Age*

them. We regard him as an experienced observer of the laws of character, which he states with insight and understanding of their inevitable results.

I do not wish to claim that there are no such laws or that they are not in accord with Jesus' standards, but I do protest that such thinking is a far remove from Jesus' mind. For Jesus, the pure in heart shall see God, not *ipso facto,* but because God will vouchsafe to them the beatific vision. The blessing is personally bestowed as a reward. In like manner whatever threats or warnings are set by Jesus before his hearers are thought of as inevitable not because he could see the working of cause and effect in the world of moral influences but because he felt sure that God would certainly manage to punish the wicked. Jesus, like the Old Testament prophets, in his predictions is not enunciating impersonal moral laws. He has no thought of tertiary causes as though God had set up a system which automatically brought disaster on the wicked and blessing on the good. Retribution is personally directed and controlled, even when it seems undiscriminating, for it is God who rains on the just and the unjust and is kind to the ungrateful and the evil.

Whenever we omit the personal agency in Jesus' thinking we probably misrepresent him. Evil brings its own disaster only through God's notice and action. Of course one may feel sure that if men are bad enough

God will do something about it. In this sense weather signs are a good illustration. But neither the decline of empires nor the losing of an individual soul is for Jesus the kind of automatic decay that moral historians and psychologists delight to expound. When men grow worse and worse it is God deliberately allowing them to hang themselves.

This conscious will of a personal agency is of course the explanation of the apocalyptic interpretation of the future of which mention has been already made. But it goes much further into Jesus' thinking and, as we shall see, determines his religion. But even when his thoughts are not so much religious as ethical, historical and practical, it provides a characteristically unmechanical environment to all that he said and thought.

That he believed as sincerely and definitely in divine servants or angels and in the sinister supernatural personal forces we have every reason to take for granted. Such allusions as we have to Satan and the demons in the gospels differ from allusions to God and the angels at most in frequency—not in literalness or assurance of belief. Though the gospel material is not abundant it is consistent and even more unwelcome to much modern liberal theology. Belief in God is still considered edifying even by those who quite unconsciously combine it with a maximum degree of mechanistic interpretation of life, but belief in Satan in any personal

CHAP. IV  *Jesus and the Mentality of Our Age*

sense is only just sporadically reviving in a few quarters in modern thought.

From the viewpoint of this unchallenged and undiluted theism of Jesus we must consider his miracles, or at least his own attitude towards them. Characteristically, modern study of the gospels regards Jesus as comparatively indifferent to his own miracles, attributes to him a kind of impatience with the evidential treatment of them by his admirers, and suggests that his own emphasis (like ours today) was upon his teaching. His reporters as usual are made the scapegoats, though they are supposed in spite of themselves to have allowed certain hints to come through. Thus Mark's story is cited: after various cures Jesus, retiring to pray in a desert place, is overtaken by Simon Peter and others who say, "All are seeking thee," to which Jesus replies, "Let us go elsewhere into the next towns that I may preach there also; for to this end came I forth." Surely this is not intended to contrast Peter's desire for more cures with Jesus' intention of more preaching, but is rather a choice between two possible scenes of action—the city where he had just been or the next towns to it.[3] Another favorite evidence is the remark of Jesus against the seeking or giving of "signs." "An evil generation seeketh after a sign but there shall be no sign given it." It is true that in the Fourth Gospel "sign" does mean what the other gospels called his mighty works, but

*The Peril of Modernizing Jesus*      CHAP. IV

surely the synoptic writers must be including here a saying with some different bearing. The sign which Jesus refuses is not his cures of the sick but some more specific miracle connected with the coming Messiah or Kingdom of God. It is difficult to be more definite about it, but I feel sure the saying belongs with the warnings against false apocalyptic.

I am far from denying that the evangelists from the earliest of them glorified the miraculous in Jesus and that both they and the oral traditions before them tended to enhance the supernatural in transmission. But that Jesus' contemporaries or Jesus himself entertained any essentially different attitude seems to me most doubtful. They all shared, in contrast with us moderns, much the same ancient viewpoint. And Jesus himself unblushingly appealed to the mighty works that he did in answering John the Baptist's question, in addressing his fellow townsmen,[4] in condemning Capernaum, Chorazin and Bethsaida and the men of his generation in general, and in refuting the charge of collusion with Beelzebub.

We may note as a mark of their contemporary character how closely the earliest miracle stories approximate the form of stories told elsewhere at the time. This applies not merely to the literary form of the stories but also to the contents. Jesus uses the same methods as the wonder-working magicians. Mark especially does not hesitate to mention his use of saliva, much as it was used by the emperor Vespasian at Alexandria, the manipulation of the affected parts with his hands, and the physical raising of the sick prior to recovery. Not only with demon cases but there particularly we get the accompaniments of exorcism—the rebuke of fever, the perhaps technical ἐμβριμάομαι, the command (twice in Mark) "be muzzled," the learning by Jesus of the demon's name and the counter effort of the demons to resist by proclaiming their knowledge of Jesus' identity. It is noteworthy that, of the four instances in Mark where the actual Aramaic words spoken by Jesus are retained, two were his words of cure, and two his words of prayer.[5] It is precisely in such matters that ancient magic and religion were interested in the *verba ipsissima*—the more barbarous and foreign the better.

One difference must be noted in Jesus' attitude to miracles which differentiates him not only from modern scientifically minded unbelievers but also from modern conservative believers. To both modern groups miracle has a meaning which it could never have to prescientific minds. For the modern man in the street miracle is the breaking of a law of nature. I know this is not an exact definition and the cautious theologian will express the matter in a very much more elaborate way. But what I want simply to say is that the rise of the scientific viewpoint has changed the meaning of a miraculous event even for those who believe in it. To the ancient theist, innocent of the rigid concepts of natural law, mechanical cause and effect, for whom God is habitually intervening and controlling things, the mighty works of Jesus were specially striking evidences of divine attention and power.

To the modern theist the miracles mean much more than the capricious exceptions in a somewhat regularly ordered world. They are the unique violation by God of the fixed laws that he has established, a special direct intervention in an otherwise largely automatic universe. So a genuine raising of the dead has for an unscientific age not merely readier credence but a more religious aspect, while in a scientific age it involves, when believed, the denial or at least a challenge of the current mechanistic philosophy. Of course it sometimes is accepted merely as an evidence of other laws beyond and above the laws we know. But in any case the gospel miracles, whether believed or disbelieved, are fitted into a different mental outlook in our day from anything which Jesus knew.

I have spoken of Jesus' apocalyptic outlook and his theism. With both of these our modern evolutionary thinking, both past and future, is in conflict, and with a true instinct the modern conservative objects to the teaching of evolution. Not merely with Genesis does

CHAP. IV  *Jesus and the Mentality of Our Age*

evolutionary philosophy conflict. It is contrary to the whole thought method of Jesus and his time. Perhaps the idea of growth is an inevitable conception for men to apply outside the obvious living objects. But the genetic interpretation of history both past and future is relatively exceptional and modern. Neither Jesus nor his contemporaries shared or could understand for example such conceptions as the growth of the Hebrew religion, the development of the ritual, the evolution of monotheism of which modern students of the Old Testament speak so readily and naturally. A modern theist can adjust these conceptions in a kind of mediate way to a notion of a personal God. But for the ancient Jew, history was a series of events under the free will of man or God and not under biological evolutionary forces, economic determinism, impersonal moral necessity, or cultural development. The fundamentalist differs of course from Jesus in that he has at least in caricature considered the idea of evolution and deliberately rejected it, while for Jesus the whole approach, either consciously or indirectly, never entered the mind. The Bible's own interpretation of life as distinct from our reconstruction of its history is not an evolutionary interpretation.

I hope the illustrations given are sufficient to suggest that Jesus' conformity to the mentality of his age spells at the same time his alienness to our own. Other examples could be given and some of them will appear in subsequent chapters, but the lesson is already plain—the need of great circumspection and rigid historical imagination in trying to conjecture in any accurate way what manner of man he was. The modern biography is only intermittently successful. To claim oneself to be rid of modern presuppositions or prejudices, whether general or personal, would be itself a mark of great prejudice. The only hope is to put plainly before us the task and its difficulties. Perhaps we shall seem thereby to ignore the individuality of Jesus in his environment, and the essential unity of mind and spirit among the great personalities of all ages. We do not belittle either of these factors, but those aspects where Jesus differed from the thought of his age, and those aspects wherein he resembles great men of other times, do not appear to be identical with each other. Still less do they with any certainty agree with those traits which we attribute to him when, in a self-flattering way, we admire him as a man ahead of his time, or in accord with our own standards. The historical Jesus as distinct from the idealized or mystical Christ shared not only our common humanity but the temporal humanity of his age. "Of like passions with ourselves" could be said of him with more fullness of truth in the first century than in the twentieth. Whatever he achieved was not because he escaped or transcended in some miracu-

CHAP. IV  *Jesus and the Mentality of Our Age*

lous way the limitations of his age, but because his impress and influence operated within them or in spite of them. Loyalty does not require a present follower to force himself into the same moulds of thought; indeed, to do so is scarcely possible, though many conservative or fundamentalist Christians make heroic efforts in that direction. An imitation of Christ that imitates the first century ideas of history and nature is no more demanded than one that imitates the contemporary Galilean diet and clothing of Jesus. Historical study and any Christianity that claims to be based on history require us to attempt to examine and understand the very unmodern viewpoint of that first century Jew by whose title we are called, and to start but not to conclude our history of Christian thought with the mind of Jesus, as nearly as we can recover it.

Chapter V

# LIMITATIONS OF JESUS' SOCIAL TEACHING

NO ONE can deal with any phase of the records of Jesus' words without acknowledging that they present but a slender basis for a systematic understanding of his thought. Whether the topic investigated be religion or ethics, Judaism or the Kingdom of God, inner character or outer conduct, Jesus' words are but *disjecta membra*. Perhaps he never spoke systematically, logically developing a single theme at some length. At any rate what he did say has come down to us in greatly condensed form—a few aphorisms, comments or parables; that is all.

A further difficulty that dogs the investigator at every point concerns the accuracy of the transmission. How far do the words recorded in Greek after some decades represent the words originally spoken in Aramaic? Have not the interests and prejudices of the followers of Jesus colored his sayings in several definite directions?

CHAP. V  *Limitations of Jesus' Social Teaching*

In the case of Jesus' ethical teaching two further limitations are suggested by the apocalyptic outlook of the gospels. Whether this horizon is due to Jesus himself or to his reporters many believe that the validity of his advice is impaired thereby. The criticism takes two different and contradictory forms. The first is the charge that Jesus' words are utopian and unpractical, indeed are meant to be, since they do not deal with living in the world that is, but are counsels of perfection for the Kingdom of God. On this ground the Christian church has often been willing to follow Jesus afar off, or to count his sayings foolishness in order to find his significance not in his words but in his person and his cosmic work of redemption.

A different objection to Jesus' ethics has resulted from the more recent recognition of eschatology in the gospels. Instead of being advice for the millennium, the sayings of Jesus are understood by consistent eschatologists as advice for the brief interim before it. They are therefore of no more value for a prolonged period of human life on this earth than when they are regarded as laws for the heavenly City of God. Emergency legislation, like utopian rules, should not be expected to apply to our slow moving and continuing human society. Jesus spoke as though he were warning contemporaries of Noah and Lot, not speaking to late-born epigoni of a twentieth Christian century like us,

*The Peril of Modernizing Jesus*     CHAP. V

"the heirs of all the ages in the foremost files of time."

These limitations of Jesus' teaching are generally reckoned with by modern scholars. The incompleteness of our records, the uncertainness of their transmission, the original inchoateness of their presentation are all admitted. Jesus laid down no rules to be universally applied; his teaching was casual and illustrative, *ad hoc* and particular. Nevertheless we are told that there is enough clear evidence to assert that he had an intense interest in human society and gave utterance to fundamental social principles which accord with the best findings of modern sociology and were intended as guidance for the revision of human relationships. His gospel was in brief a social gospel. "The Kingdom of God," said Walter Rauschenbusch, "is the lost social ideal of Christianity." Even the apocalyptic element in his teaching can be adjusted to this verdict. It can be put off on Jesus' reporters or it can be admitted to Jesus himself without serious interference with the ideal of him as a social teacher. The apocalyptic element in him was part of the unavoidable husk of Judaism, but it was without influence on the essential inner message. Jesus' social teaching was based on timeless principles—applicable alike to the millennium and the premillennium —so that while logically he should have been biased by the consideration of the difference between the real present and the ideal future, between *Interimsethik* and

CHAP. V  *Limitations of Jesus' Social Teaching*

the standards for an evolving civilization, practically, i.e., psychologically, he lived and taught others to live as though the kingdom had already come—obliterating these distinctions.

The limitations which I have mentioned are, however, all quite minor as compared with the objection which I wish to raise in this chapter to the modern emphasis on Jesus' social teaching. The fundamental question is: Did Jesus really have a social outlook at all? The answer to this question depends on how one defines "social." Probably it can be defined in such a way as to be applicable to Jesus. The word has a breadth of meaning and I do not wish to quibble about words. But as the term is commonly used today there seems a strange excess, not to say anachronism, in so strongly connecting Jesus with its various connotations.

The vogue of the social interpretation of the gospel is familiar even to a superficial observer of tendencies in religious thought. In one sense it is a new thought which in America at least dates from the familiar books from near the beginning of this century by Professors Peabody, Rauschenbusch and Mathews. It has become part of the newer orthodoxy of liberal Christianity and has seeped into all the crannies of Christian influence, in the church and out of it, including the unchurched masses of labor, the youth and radical movements, as well as ecclesiastical bodies with their

## The Peril of Modernizing Jesus   CHAP. V

social programs or "creeds" and social service. As a natural development of Christian thought it is doubtless inevitable, as a corrective for wrong perspectives it has been valuable, as a hope for future achievement it is most promising. But for historical students the question remains: How far did Jesus of Nazareth really share the modern viewpoint?

We are only too prone to criticize the past generations for making Jesus in their own image. The tendency to do so we cannot escape ourselves, but the twentieth century is not so justified in representing Jesus as a sociological expert as the sixth century was in painting him as an ascetic or monk. We at least pride ourselves on an honest effort at historical perspective and imagination. For an age that boasts of scientific history, anachronism is a more unpardonable sin. To make of the scriptures mere echoes of our passing styles of thought, which will render us the answers which we want them to give, is to imitate the servile oracles of the pagans which answered to suit the wishes of the inquirers. It behooves us to examine anew the evidence for the social definition of the gospel of Jesus.

The grounds for a social understanding of Jesus' message are usually three—first and most explicitly, his instruction to social acts, as loving, forgiving, giving, and his warning against their opposites; second, his own example as one who went about doing good

CHAP. V   *Limitations of Jesus' Social Teaching*

to those who were diseased in mind, body or estate, who came not to be waited on but to wait on others and to give his life a ransom for many. Third, much stress is laid also on the terms of his teaching.

It is obviously unnecessary, or if necessary impossible, to review all this evidence. Let me call attention to the last item as an illustration of the socializing of the gospel, and quote some passages from Shailer Mathews in his book on the *Social Teaching of Jesus:*

The central thought of Jesus is usually associated with the terms Kingdom of God and God as Father. Though Jesus rejected for the former the particularistic ambition of his countrymen, he retained, we are told, its social meaning and made it the expression of an ideal social order, based upon character. Of the Fatherhood of God it is also observed that it is a social as well as a religious relationship and that it involves genealogically the inference that all men are brothers. The invocation "our father" includes us all in reciprocal brotherhood and gives expression even at the inception of our personal devotion to the social implications of the gospel.

For the Kingdom of God Professor Mathews after discussing and rejecting various other possible meanings gives his own definition—fortified in a footnote by quotations from Seeley, Bruce, Keim, Edersheim, Stead, Weiss, Candlish, Beyschlag and Denney—as follows:

## The Peril of Modernizing Jesus  CHAP. V

By the Kingdom of God Jesus meant *an ideal* (though progressively approximated) *social order in which the relation of men to God is that of sons and* (therefore) *to each other, that of brothers.*

Although Jesus sometimes refers especially to the dominion of God in his kingdom, he generally keeps prominent the social conception.

The analogies with which this . . . kingdom is described are full of social signification. As in its very genesis the term denoted social relations, so is it a net, a great feast, a family, into each of which men enter and from which they may be excluded.

This conclusion that by the kingdom of God Jesus meant a society, is confirmed by the position which the kingdom as the ideal occupies in relation to the world, as the actual social order.

In the old social order Jesus saw the tyranny of selfishness and hatred; in the new, he sees a universal reign of love—the fatherhood of God and the brotherhood of men. This expression, the fatherhood of God and the brotherhood of men, is in many minds the substance of Christianity. And such is the case if these terms are given their proper meaning.

The entrance into a transformed society is the goal and the reward of the individual's endeavor. . . . The unideal, the abnormal, the sinful condition of mankind . . . may be described as one of unsocial relationships. . . . Sin is the reverse of sociability. . . . In failing to follow the fundamental instincts and capacities of his nature, a man becomes at once selfish, unsocial, and sinful. . . . Hell is thus at once the opposite and the horrible caricature of heaven, for it is

CHAP. V    *Limitations of Jesus' Social Teaching*

not merely an accommodation of his thought to Jewish terminology when Jesus describes the selfish rich man as suffering alone in Gehenna, and the poor man as in the companionship of Abraham.[1]

The sound of these sentences is familiar; but when attention is called to such passages the interpreter's excess is readily perceived. It is purely gratuitous to suppose that Dives was alone in Hades. He does not complain of solitude but of torment and in any case he expected five brothers for company soon. If we may judge from the saying of the strait gate and the narrow way the lonely place is heaven.[2] The other parables are also overweighted when made to yield social evidence.

Even the brotherhood of men in any abstract sense is not explicit in the gospels. It is derived of course from the fatherhood of God, but it is modern writers who make the step of inference by a literal understanding of Father.[3] Jesus does not connect the brotherhood of men with God, perhaps he does not use the idea at all. If he does occasionally refer to a man and his brother there is no reason to suppose he is passing beyond the confines of actual physical brotherhood or the simple Semitic idiom by which brother means "fellow" or co-religionist, or another man, or B as distinct from A.

It is particularly dangerous to stress the terms of

*The Peril of Modernizing Jesus*  CHAP. V

Jesus. They are the most conventional part of his teaching and the least rather than the most significant. Etymologically and historically they may have had social meaning. Both the fatherhood and the Kingdom of God are apparently fixed inheritances; they are probably religious metaphors from human social life, as indeed are most religious terms, but there is no evidence that Jesus brought back into them human social connotations. Even religiously the fatherhood of God is neither a novelty nor a new emphasis with Jesus.[4] If, as seems likely, the Kingdom of God is a time word —the reign of God—its social meaning is even more remote than if it had been a borrowed Jewish name for a utopian place or community. Terms, especially borrowed terms, prove but little. Individualistic ideals can be described in terms primarily social and vice versa, just as the absolute despotism of God's Kingdom (see the parables) is now construed to mean Jeffersonian democracy.[5]

As to Jesus' message and the motives of his own conduct, a similar tendency to import modern social ideas is displayed in much that is said and written nowadays. Perhaps no further illustration of these excesses is necessary. The Social Gospel, which meets such coolness from continental theologians generally, has for a generation been the staple diet of American liberals. From every college pulpit, in every church

CHAP. V    *Limitations of Jesus' Social Teaching*

conference it has been proclaimed as *the* gospel of Jesus. Professor Mathews, whom I have quoted, is merely one of its earliest spokesmen. The universality of it is manifest.

Now our main purpose is not to show that others have misrepresented Jesus but rather to indicate that the most authentic gospel material itself betrays in the teaching of Jesus what from the standpoint of modern social thinking must seem to be serious limitations. I shall mention four of these.

1. *Social Institutions.* In the first place the records suggest that Jesus rarely if ever dealt with social institutions as such. The modern Christian asks what is the ethics of human customs or conventions, like government, taxation, tariff, war, slavery, private property, inheritance of wealth, interest on money, monogamy, prostitution, racial discrimination. We find it hard to believe that Jesus did not think of some of these questions from the same angle as we do—not of individual ethics merely but of social ethics. The phenomena were all existent in his day. Most of them are mentioned somewhere in his sayings. The fact that he consorts with soldiers, tax collectors, harlots and even a Roman centurion suggests that he had some knowledge of many of these professions. That he mentions without criticism in parables slaveholders, capitalists, monarchs, and tax collectors has been thought by some to indi-

cate that he had reflected on the morality of these institutions and had at least by his silence endorsed them. But the fact of the matter is he had probably never thought of them in that way. The question of taxation was for him at most the specific question of Jews paying taxes to Rome rather than the question of tax collecting and tax paying in general. It is not irreverent to suppose that the modern ethical problems—of chattel slavery, war, competitive business—no more entered Jesus' head in the modern form than they did the heads of his contemporaries and of his followers for many centuries. And for questions which he did not raise, his silence does not mean consent. His judgment dealt with individuals rather than with the organized life in which they lived. On some of these points there may have been a prevailing standard which he unconsciously shared—either of traditional moral judgment or non-moral necessity. In saying "The poor ye have always with you," he did not approve the uneven distribution of wealth by the method of private property any more than he condemned it in saying, "Woe unto you rich." The social acts which Judaism had condemned Jesus doubtless condemned—murder, theft, adultery—but that is not the same as saying that he had approved as social institutions the inalienable rights of a man to wife, life and property.

An apparent exception to this position of Jesus is in

CHAP. V  *Limitations of Jesus' Social Teaching*

his saying about divorce or, more properly described, his saying about divorce and the remarriage of divorced persons. The differences of the four passages in the gospels are well known and illustrate how fortunate it is that Jesus' teaching did not usually take the form of social legislation. Though we may not know precisely what Jesus prescribed, apparently he is to be thought of here as expressing an opinion on the Mosaic institution of divorce or at least on the second marriage of divorcés. In view of the absence of reliable parallels, this case must remain a conspicuous though illuminating exception.[6]

2. *Social Groups.* Another difference between the viewpoint of Jesus and the modern social viewpoint, as far as we can observe the former, is his indifference to the solidarity of society and to the treatment of society as of one or more units. Classes he knew, races, sexes, etc.; but apparently not class interests, class consciousness, class ideals. In some ways this absence of the group concept in Jesus' thinking seems remarkable. The older Judaism was a national religion and, in spite of the increasing individualism since the Exile, can scarcely have divested itself of all the elements of group feeling, political, racial, social and religious. Jesus can view men in their actual contacts but scarcely in what we call their mystical unity or even in collective coöperation. However much he may use col-

lective names, his thinking is not wholesale but individual. The individual may be a type, there may be groups of typical individuals; but the social group, social solidarity as we conceive it, is not an abstraction attributable to Jesus.

Preachers of the modern social gospel deny this limitation with special vigor. Revolting from the individualism of theology they affirm with one voice that society, not individuals merely, is the subject of redemption. Charles A. Ellwood in his *Reconstruction of Religion* writes:

> The distinctive note of Christianity was "redemption"—not simply of the individual but of the world. For it looked to the establishment of a social order in which the divine will should be realized—"a Kingdom of God." But Jesus did not conceive that this Utopia could be created merely by changes in individual souls without moral conflicts in the external social order.
>
> Positive Christianity will be collective rather than individualistic. An ethical Christianity must necessarily make the community, indeed, as much its concern as the individual, since the conditions of the community surely determine in greater or less degree the individual life. The world is the subject of redemption for positive Christianity. There is every warrant for believing that this was the attitude of Jesus. The Kingdom of God which he announced he had come to establish is essentially a social conception meaning an order of human society.

CHAP. V  *Limitations of Jesus' Social Teaching*

We find Jesus saying little concerning individual personality, but much concerning his ideal society. While he regarded each human soul as of infinite worth, yet it was of worth because it was part of an ideal society, a part of a spiritual kingdom which was to come fully only when the world was redeemed and God's will was done upon the earth. An ideal human world was to him the goal of religion.[7]

So Ellwood and many of his kind, some of whom he quotes. They must not only rescue the phrase Kingdom of God from the perversions of older theologians but also detach it from Schweitzer and other eschatologists, whose view is equally opposed to the social conception of Christianity.

As a matter of fact I think this form of social emphasis has turned our gospels the wrong way around. No doubt there were social implications and social results in the advice that Christ gave to individuals. But his aim was the unit and not the mass. General improvement could be at most a by-product of personal right behavior, not vice versa. Even when he gave advice to crowds or pointed out the faults of groups like the Pharisees, his concern was for personal repentance and reform.

3. *Social Interrelation.* When we follow Jesus to the simplest inter-personal situation some modern social attitudes are lacking. In a mutual relationship the

*The Peril of Modernizing Jesus*            CHAP. V

modern mind tries to deal with both parties at once and to rise into a plane or principle of action which takes the interests, privileges, rights or duties of both into view. Jesus appears conversely to think of one man at a time, and if some modern man should say, as reported of Peter, "What shall this man do?" his reply would be, "What is that to thee? follow thou me." When a pair of brothers are in dispute over inherited property Jesus declines to arbitrate, but he will advise the brother before him against his own covetousness. In the parable of the workers in the vineyard Jesus seems almost to flout this idea of a uniformly applicable principle. Their wages are not proportionate to their hours of labor. Where the characters are not in parallel positions like fellow employees but in diverse relations, as in the parable of the prodigal son, each of the three figures is expected to behave not by some reciprocal principle or compensating or unifying law, but each quite independently as his own situation demands. There is there at least no thought of father's forgiveness contingent on son's repentance or vice versa. The older son's complaint is answered much as is that of the laborers who had borne the burden and heat of the day. The slave is not to expect even thanks from his master for his one-sided service. Perhaps the sayings of Jesus contain certain suggestions of principles, mostly of proportion or parallelism.

CHAP. V  *Limitations of Jesus' Social Teaching*

To whom much is committed of him shall much be required.
To whom little is forgiven the same loveth little.
He that is faithful in a very little is faithful also in much.
If ye forgive not, God will not forgive you.⁸

These are, however, arguments *a fortiori,* or by analogy. But these are very far from principles of respective duty, balancing opposing factors or plotting triangular solutions or complementary relationships like any modern social principle. Even the Golden Rule is not bifocal in its intention but merely advice for each man by himself. The sense of interaction in Kant's famous dictum, "So act that the law of thy action should become universal," is lacking in the words of Jesus.

4. *Social Motive.* Much the most striking of all the conspicuous absences in Jesus' teaching when compared with modern social thinking has yet to be mentioned: the appeal to social motive.

The motives and sanctions in Jesus' ethics have, so far as I know, never been thoroughly studied, and I am not prepared at this point to supply what would no doubt make an interesting monograph. The motives to which Jesus appeals are varied. Sometimes he appeals to no motive at all, demanding a self-sacrifice that asks no return, counts not the cost—a kind of spontaneous goodness. At other times he appeals to men's own sense of what is right, the axiomatic self-

## The Peril of Modernizing Jesus — CHAP. V

evidence of virtuous standards. In a few passages he is represented as urging a religious motive, "that men seeing your good works may glorify your father which is in heaven," or dedication to a person or a cause, "for Christ's sake and the gospel's." Frequently the only motive apparent is what we now would call a self-regarding motive, but nowhere—and this is my point—do I find unmistakable appeal to the rights or needs of the other party or even to the interests of society in general.

Now we shall probably all agree that of the modern social gospel the altruistic appeal is the great conscious factor. What is known as social work, for example, claims the devotion of thousands of workers on the ground of human need. The modern slogan, often indeed sordidly corrupted in self-seeking business interests, is "service." The misfortune, sickness, poverty or ignorance of our fellow men, women and children not only touches our heart but calls forth what we account a characteristically Christian humanitarianism of conscious purpose.

It is natural, therefore, that we should read this motive into the words and deeds of Jesus. Let me indicate, however, some instances where this motive is conspicuously absent.

We read constantly, for example, that Jesus taught the infinite worth of the human soul in the sight of

CHAP. V  *Limitations of Jesus' Social Teaching*

God and that we also ought to count men precious. The proof passage is probably, "Ye are of more value than many sparrows, etc." But it is you who are of value, not some other man whom you are reminded not to injure. Nowhere does Jesus restrain evil doing by reference to the other man's rights or interests. He does not suggest that hate or murder, unforgivingness, censoriousness, and the like are hard or unpleasant or unfair to the other man. No doubt it is a pity that little ones should be made to stumble, but woe to that man through whom the offenses come. Jesus is not thinking of the object of the social or anti-social act, but of the doer of that act and as I have said he does not think of both parties at the same time.

An interesting illustration of this difference of viewpoint is found, if the wording may be trusted, precisely in the parable of the Good Samaritan—that patron saint of modern philanthropy. The lawyer having been told to love his neighbor asks the question "Who is my neighbor?" that is, "whom shall I befriend?" and Jesus after telling the story is represented as repeating the question in the precise reverse, "Who proved himself neighbor to him that fell among thieves?" that is, "who did the befriending?" This change of emphasis corresponds to the distinctiveness of Jesus' whole unmodern attitude towards social relations. In one case the needy and his needs, in the other the helper and

*The Peril of Modernizing Jesus*     CHAP. V

his help. The two cannot be separated but there is a difference in the point of departure in your thinking —the villain or the victim, the lover or the beloved.

I have tried in vain to find in our synoptic gospels a single injunction to social service based explicitly on the neighbor's need for love and service. When Hermann and Harnack wrote their *Essays on the Social Gospel* their best text was not from a canonical gospel but from the uncanonical Gospel of the Hebrews, where Jesus says, "Behold many of thy brethren, sons of Abraham, are clad with dung, dying with hunger and thy house is full of much goods, and there goeth out therefrom nought at all unto them." [9] In another agraphon Jesus says, "Because of the weak was I weak, and because of the hungry did I hunger, and because of the thirsty did I thirst," and in another, "Never be joyful except when ye have looked upon your brother with love." Attractive as such sayings are to us they are not from the authentic gospels.[10]

From this angle of incidence we understand the frequent references in Jesus' teaching to the self-regarding factor in a social act. His attention to the reward of philanthropy is nothing less than heresy according to the standards of modern popular altruism and is either overlooked or whittled away by many modern readers of the gospels. The mercenary idea of charity for the sake of personal return, no matter how we try

CHAP. V    *Limitations of Jesus' Social Teaching*

to sublimate the motive, we think of as Jewish or mediæval Christian rather than as typical of the gospel of Jesus. We should like to lay the responsibility for it upon the reporters of Jesus, trained in the Jewish religion of works and rewards, or if we must admit it as the genuine thought of Jesus, we deprecate it as something inferior to his higher ideals expressed in his parable of the obedient servant's renunciation of merit and elsewhere, and we suppose that perhaps he adopted it for pedagogical reasons just as we ourselves, who know better, use candy or spanking to teach ideals to children.

While the absence of altruistic motive in the synoptic gospels is an argument from silence and hence like all negative inferences confessedly precarious, the presence in them of the self-regarding factor is explicit and abundant. The forms are not always a bald purpose clause like "Judge not, in order that ye be not judged" but even other forms of syntax, such as the condition or simple statement of result, cannot be denied a similar meaning. Like "Honesty is the best policy" each statement of Jesus may be called a mere law, but scarcely an abstract law stated for disinterested contemplation without motive. So it makes very little difference which of the following grammatical forms our records actually use:

Forgive ... in order that your Father may forgive you.
Release and ye shall be released.
If ye forgive men their trespasses, your heavenly Father will also forgive you.
Forgive us our debts as we also have forgiven our debtors.
Forgive us our sins; for we ourselves also forgive everyone that is indebted to us.
Blessed are the merciful, for they shall obtain mercy.
Be ye merciful, even as your Father is merciful.[11]

In any case there is attention to the reward or at least to the standpoint of the forgiving man rather than of the man whom he forgives.

Illustrations of this fact are abundant. The commands to almsgiving frequently mention the benefit to be received by the donor rather than by the recipient. Like mercy "it blesses him that gives and him that takes," but Jesus is thinking of the donor: "it is more blessed to give than to receive." The evil of wealth is its effect upon the wealthy. They can scarcely enter the Kingdom of God. And so when the rich young man is to sell all and give to the poor, nothing is said about the poor's need, still less is considered the harm money may do the poor. Perhaps their need is taken for granted. They may need to get it, but *he* needs to get rid of it. "One thing *thou* lackest: go, sell whatever thou hast and give to the poor and thou shalt have treasure in heaven." "Sell that which ye have and give

CHAP. V  *Limitations of Jesus' Social Teaching*

alms: make for yourselves purses which wax not old, a treasure in the heavens that faileth not." As Stanton says, "The prospect of obtaining heavenly treasure in place of the earthly that is bestowed on the poor is, it will be observed, employed as a motive . . . [Luke] was not frightened by the idea that men might be encouraged to perform good works here by the hope of the hereafter." [12] Even the beautiful story of those who have fed the hungry, clothed the naked and visited the sick without thought of Christ is told in the eschatological setting of judgment and rewards—the kingdom prepared for the good, the eternal fire which is prepared for the devil and his angels. For kindness to the lame, halt and blind, unreturnable in this world, "thou shall be recompensed in the resurrection of the just."

The familiar appeal to post-mortem retribution is not the only illustration of the self-regarding motive in Jesus' teaching. Those who have left all and followed him are to have in this time a hundredfold as well as eternal life in the age to come. The more immediate returns from conduct are appealed to. Sometimes the simplest prudential motive appears for conciliation, almsgiving, humility, non-resistance.

For as thou art going with thine adversary before the magistrate, on the way give diligence to be quit of him;

lest haply he hale thee unto the judge and the judge shall deliver thee unto the officer and the officer shall cast thee into prison.

Make to yourself friends by means of the mammon of unrighteousness; that, when it shall fail, they may receive you into the eternal tabernacles.

Put up again thy sword into its place: for all they that take the sword shall perish with the sword.

When thou are bidden, go and sit down in the lowest place; that when he that hath bidden thee cometh, he may say to thee, Friend, go up higher: then shalt thou have glory in the presence of all that sit at meat with thee.[13]

Many of the sayings of Jesus used for the modern gospel of altruism are perhaps originally of the same kind. The Golden Rule does not leave out oneself. "As ye would that men should do to you" may be partly motive as well as standard. If you want something for yourself do it to others. "With what measure ye mete it shall be measured to you again." So with service—if you want to be great you must be the servant, if you would save your life you must lose it. The accent is not exclusively on the sacrifice. Professor E. F. Scott writes:

It cannot be maintained that Jesus made the social motive the primary one in the moral life. To be sure he insists continually on the need for service and sacrifice. He requires that as he came himself not to be ministered unto but to

CHAP. V   *Limitations of Jesus' Social Teaching*

minister, so his followers must look to the good of others. ... Yet the idea which underlies it [his moral demand] is always that by denying himself a man gains something for his own soul. "He that would be greatest among you, let him be the servant of all." "He that is last shall be first." "He that loseth his life shall find it." "Blessed are the poor, the meek, the peace-makers, the persecuted, for theirs is the Kingdom of Heaven." The promises of Jesus always come back to some good that will accrue not to mankind as a whole [nor, we may add, to the objects of neighborliness] but to the man himself.[14]

This "eudaemonism" of Jesus constitutes a problem in ethics which I am not disposed to enter into. It has perhaps its dangers; it has perhaps also its justification. There are various grades of selfishness, higher and lower, and Jesus was perhaps not conscious of the distinction. Montefiore thinks he blended selfishness and unselfishness, was quite innocent of the antithesis as a problem in ethical sanction, and "was not concerned to remove from his teaching the least suspicion of eudaemonism." I do not wish to defend or condemn this use of self-regarding motives. Even if you dislike the motive you do not need to condemn the advice. Sometimes sound conduct is taught on false motives. How far self-seeking is today a false motive I may leave it to experts on ethical theory to tell us.

Historically honest Protestants should be very careful not to make odious contrasts between the alleged altruism of the gospel (and of ourselves!), on the one hand, and the alleged mercenary spirit either of the rabbis with their system of works of the law and credits in heaven or of mediæval Catholicism and its bookkeeping of merits, prayers, etc., on the other.

Sometimes the contrast looks quite the other way. Jesus, for example, forbids ostentatious almsgiving done with trumpet blowings and in public places in order to be glorified by men. Now the rabbis also urge secret or inconspicuous charity. They have in mind the sensitiveness of the recipient and in many ways try to teach genuine delicacy of feelings for those who are in the embarrassing position of having to accept charity. Yet the gospel says not a word of their feelings but rather gives as its reason, "Thy Father who seeth in secret shall reward thee (openly)." [15]

What I think may be safely asserted from the evidence is that Jesus' approach to social relations is through the individual rather than the group and through the doer rather than the recipient of social service. What Montefiore says about non-resistance is applicable to other parts of Jesus' teaching. He says:

Jesus, perhaps one-sidedly, is really thinking much more of the doer than of the recipient; that is to say, *in this particular passage,* he is not thinking so much of the redemp-

CHAP. V    *Limitations of Jesus' Social Teaching*
tion of the evil doer as he is thinking of the ideal conduct for those who have to do with the evil doer, or, generally, of the ideal for man. Still less is he thinking of society as a whole and of the effect of not resisting evil upon the State.[16]

Such then are four apparent limitations of Jesus' approach to social questions. If they are true, it is important to bear them constantly in mind since men nowadays are looking so wistfully to Jesus for social guidance, and "historical perspective is a factor too often forgotten in the anxiety to state the ideas of Jesus in modern terms." The most important difference between Jesus and ourselves is not the external social conditions but the inner ways of thinking. If the silence of the gospels may be taken as suggestive of Jesus' own viewpoint, four primary concepts in modern sociological thinking were absent from his teaching—social institutions as the objects of moral criticism and control; society itself or groups in society as entities, fabrics or systems; social principles as regulative laws of mutual relationship; the social motive as an external stimulus to action. Deprived of such categories of thought such books as Ellwood's would completely fade out of existence. So far are Jesus' thoughts from our thoughts. I am not asking that we should empty our minds of the modern viewpoint. A return to the naïveté of Jesus is impossible, but an appreciation of the difference is the first duty of genuine historical study or of honest application.

Not only must we give up in general our social misunderstanding of Jesus. We must be particularly careful not to quote him as the ally and prophet of our modern social programs and reforms. There may be reasons for a modern Christian to espouse prohibition, pacifism, socialism or communism as so many liberal Christians do. But to claim Jesus as holding in any explicit, literal or conscious way such modern philosophies is the grossest anachronism. Of course by the same token the capitalists and militarists have no more right to claim him. His teaching only in the remotest way lies parallel to these modern "isms" and none of them, not even the best of them, can be wisely or safely promoted by a partisan dishonesty to the facts of history. With Jesus' general principles to guide us these are issues which in this complicated world we must judge as best we can on our own responsibility, and not seek piously to shelter ourselves behind an effigy of Christ, nor conceitedly claim a superior loyalty to him.[17]

As we thus understand him, some of the criticisms and difficulties raised by his words will disappear. We can see, for example, why the apocalyptic viewpoint which he held did not warp and pervert his ethical teaching. If anything, it intensified its correct-

CHAP. V  *Limitations of Jesus' Social Teaching*

ness. For us with our outlook on society, on social institutions, etc., the future course of history has some bearing, but the right spontaneous attitude of individuals is independent of all millenarian or evolutionist cosmologies. Apocalypticism and the gradual remaking of society are mutually irreconcilable and the modern fundamentalist is logically indifferent to sociological programs and propaganda. Jesus too was apocalyptic and we can see now that his outlook does not have to be fitted with our own hope for a slowly developing Kingdom of God. His ethical hope was not like ours. "His primary interest," says Scott quite correctly, "is not that of making the world better, for this will be accomplished by God Himself when He brings in the Kingdom, but that of fostering an active goodness in men and women." Such ethics there is no trouble in reconciling with apocalypse.

Similarly the limitations of Jesus' social outlook make intelligible many hard sayings of the Sermon on the Mount—like, "Resist not evil," "Give to everyone that asketh thee," "Be not anxious for the morrow." We are not in any sense denying their validity in explaining that they were not promulgated by Jesus as laws of perfected society, or as sociological principles, or as the therapeutic of social ills—much less as literal rules for universal conduct. But when one sees that Jesus is trying to illustrate simply and solely how a man of soundest instincts and motives ought to react to varied circumstances, these and similar so-called hyperbolic commands are most illuminating. So far from being the extreme of ethical perfection to be outwardly aspired to, they are the natural results of a right inner spirit that follow without effort.

An understanding of Jesus' social outlook affects the application of his teaching. Indeed, Jesus' teaching can be much more easily used than if it had been directed to questions of social organization. The laborious task of deducing Jesus' message for modern society as the fourth term in the proportion in which one must first know accurately the three terms: modern society, first century Palestinian society, and Jesus' judgments concerning it, is not so necessary. Moffatt, in his *Approach to the New Testament,* repeatedly stresses the difficulty of interpreting Jesus' meaning about divorce, trade, property and politics compared with forgiveness and prayer. He says, "The spiritual phenomena of the inward life are much more readily seized by the imagination of today working sympathetically upon the New Testament than the cognate references to social ethics, for the social setting has altered so radically that the latter require very careful study if their permanent value is to be estimated." [18] But the difficulty is not so great if Jesus' social teaching began, after all, with the phenomena of the inward life and worked outward

CHAP. V *Limitations of Jesus' Social Teaching*
and if it was not adjusted specially to fit a temporary social setting. Perhaps one can ascertain his simple social technique quite directly: "Make the tree good."

Jesus' way is often criticized as idealistic, as though it began with the ideal and failed to take account of the *status quo*. In a sense this criticism is quite wrong way around. Jesus begins with the individual man where he is and tells him what to do. It is the modern mind that starts with the ideal to be realized and inquires the steps by which it can be reached. Many who today commend Jesus' teaching do so from the quite modern ground that it will lead to the ideal social order. It is doubtful whether this appeal has power to produce the character that Jesus commends on other motives. The religion of Jesus may bring peace of mind, peace in society, sanity, health and prosperity as the sociological advocates for Christianity expect, but they need not count on these ambitions or the fear of their opposites as the motives that will create a revived Christianity. It is doubtful whether true Christianity can be promoted as men nowadays try to promote other crusades. The "selling talk" of modern salesmanship may be useful in political and social reform, but with all its appeal to anticipated public advantages it differs from the most selfish-sounding motives in the gospels.

An appreciation of the limitations of Jesus' social

teaching gives not only a more accurate historical view. It suggests certain practical advantages of his method, to which possibly we may return with profit.

By his emphasis upon the doer of good rather than the recipient of good, upon the perpetrator of evil rather than the victim of evil, Jesus seems to rely on man's sense of duty rather than his sense of rights. Moral responsibility rather than a claim for justice is the motive for righteousness. Jesus' concern is not so much the saving of society but a society of saviors, not the reduction of victims of brigandage on the Jerusalem-Jericho road but the multiplication of good Samaritans. It has been scornfully said that if Jesus were alive now he would substitute for his parable of the good Samaritan a plan for electric street lights between Jerusalem and Jericho. This may be the modern substitute but it is not the method of Jesus. The modern reliance on laws, reforms, changed customs, mechanical preventives does not make obsolete Jesus' method. It has been truly said that Jesus believed that character should transform environment, not vice versa, and there are many times when the greater wisdom and permanence of his method are manifest.

There is another advantage for those who begin like Jesus with correct individual reaction rather than with an ultimate ideal society. They need not rely on the guidance of expediency and conjectured results, nor

CHAP. V    *Limitations of Jesus' Social Teaching*

are they tempted to adopt immoral means to worthy ends. One of the tragedies of so much moral idealism of modern society is precisely here that, with its eye on right through distant goals, it allows itself to follow paths which themselves ignore or deny the same ideals. Hence we crush the individual in order to make a better world for individuals, we permit tyranny in the quest of liberty, we wage wars to end war. Were we as sensitive to the immediate consistency of the means as we are ambitious for the ends, we might discover that evil is not the road to good.

Nor is Jesus' interest in the individual instead of in society altogether undesirable—calling the sinners instead of the righteous, leaving the ninety and nine to seek the one lost sheep. No theologian has more clearly discovered this antinomy than a popular writer named H. H. Powers in an article called "A Question for Christians" in *The Atlantic Monthly* a few years ago. After discussing Jesus' saying to the woman taken in adultery, "Neither do I condemn thee," as well as his teaching on non-resistance and "no thought for the morrow," he says:

This is but one of many indications that Jesus refused to recognize the organic character of society, a doctrine upon which Paul laid the greatest emphasis and one which is fundamental in the social philosophy of our time. He insists upon regarding primarily the individual and in claiming salvage for the salvable, irrespective of social reactions. He distinctly enunciates this policy in the well-known words, later fantastically denaturalized by theological interpretation: "The Son of Man is come to seek and to save that which was lost." In a word, He stands for individual salvage, while conservative society has always stood for social quarantine. Confronted with a victim of moral contagion, He urges that the case can be cured, to which society replies: "Yes, but with cost and risks which we cannot afford to incur."

The words of Jesus with all their mistaken disparagement of thrift and injunction to unlimited charity, are words that do Him honor. Their very extravagance demonstrates the splendid passion for humanity which prompted their utterance.... I claim for Jesus the glorious economic irresponsibility of the idealist and the prophet.[19]

Powers plainly thinks society right and Jesus wrong and justifies the Christian in honoring him without obeying him. There is still something to be said on Jesus' side.

A return to Jesus would mean a return in part at least to the religious motive, the religious attitude with which his advice is inseparably connected even when it seems to be the least altruistic. No passion for humanity, no philanthropic sentiment, no program for social betterment can be more effective in producing perfectly socialized persons than the essentially reli-

CHAP. V     *Limitations of Jesus' Social Teaching*

gious spirit such as we find in Jesus. This religious spirit cannot be put on at will, is not always easy for the modern mind. In fact it must be expressed in different terms in different ages and may today sometimes lurk unrecognized or scornfully denied under the philosophy of sociology and philanthropy. When it does exist it is marked by the same power, insight, instinctive virtue and persistent efficacy which marked the career of Jesus, though by all modern efficiency standards that career seems to the philanthropists a stumbling block and to the sociologists foolishness.

Chapter VI

# PURPOSE, AIM AND MOTIVE IN JESUS

ONE of the assumptions that we make of any man, especially of a great man whose intelligence and success we admire, is that he was possessed of a clear and well chosen purpose in life. Of course we recognize that circumstances interfere with the pursuit of a single aim, at least that the method has to be sometimes adjusted to the possibilities in the case. But opportunist behavior is not incompatible with a steady underlying purpose. Probably we recognize also that, in our own time and in the past as well, this unifying principle is often less determinative than it seems to the actor. It may be for him a rationalizing of temperamental or circumstantial factors. But it seems to us inconceivable that the question should not present itself to him and should not hold the key to the secret of his life. The person's aim is to be deduced from his recorded words and actions. These words and actions were motivated by his aim. They were chosen

CHAP. VI     *Purpose, Aim and Motive in Jesus*

with a view to their effectiveness towards the end that was conceived. Thus each consistent individual represents a natural interrelation of a general aim, of corresponding particular motives, and of reactions according with that aim and those motives.

This assumption of the modern man is inevitably applied in writing and thinking about Jesus. It is indeed more assumed than affirmed but it colors none the less most biographical efforts.[1] As to what his aim was there may be much difference of opinion; one would suppose that there would be available books and articles comparing proposed aims and objectives of his life. That is, however, not the case. The one book that professes in its title to consider *The Aim of Jesus* is concerned to present only the author's own understanding of it.[2] Other volumes also each weave their portrait about some imagined purpose.

My intention here is not to compare the aims assigned to him. To do so would be a long and elaborate study, especially with the many modern lives of Christ. I must admit that many of these books gain in force and lifelikeness by their adopting of the unifying element of a definite purpose in the portrait of Jesus. Indeed, several of the most effective of them have owed their effect to just this trait. To mention but a single example, one recalls the influential volume of Henry Latham's issued in 1890 called *Pastor Pastorum*. Here the life of Christ was interpreted as a great educational undertaking, the training of the twelve. The events of Jesus' life were brought into an intelligible pattern, with a farsighted plan and well chosen actions.

In all such books, so different in character, we have the common element of an interpretation of Jesus through relating him to an aim. The more definite and conscious that aim and the more completely it is shown to dominate his life, the more clear a pattern it seems to give to the scattered memorabilia of the gospels and the more real it seems to make their hero. Whether the aim is correctly divined or not is another question. Obviously not all of the aims proposed can be alike true. For the essence of the concept is that the aim should be inclusive of all facts and exclusive of all other possible aims.

The question that now is raised is not which of these portraits is true, as if we could reject one by the adoption of another. It is rather the prior question, the assumption that all of them have in common, that some rather definite objective lies at the root of Jesus' career. Was Jesus, after all, not so modern and so purposive as we assume? Naturally we cannot disprove this modern assumption from the records. There are, however, some *a priori* considerations worth mentioning.

Like most of the rest of us, Jesus was born into a culture that was a going concern. Few Jews had any occa-

CHAP. VI    *Purpose, Aim and Motive in Jesus*

sion to reflect upon the purpose of human life in general or of their own lives in particular. Their religion gave an answer to any who were inquisitive, just as the Christian creeds did for a later inquirer into "the whole duty of man." Above all, example and convention gave the main direction to lives. There was for each a path of least resistance. They followed a normal round from birth to death. To plot a career *de novo* would occur to almost nobody. Just when did self-consciousness of career really develop fully in human history? I suspect it to be of Puritan rather than of primitive Jewish vintage. It is perhaps associated with the idea of a divine calling, which no doubt has its origin in the old Hebrew prophets, but which in its economic aspects is believed to be connected with the Protestant interpretation of man's labor and profession.[3]

Of course, in Jesus' day too there were professions and trades. To a large extent these set the pattern. A builder by trade, he would in that trade follow certain lines of natural development, varied, of course, by his own peculiar circumstances and interests. But in his adult life Jesus did not rely on this trade. Unlike our modern culture his was not an age of almost coercive need to make a living. Steady employment, economic regularity of daily program, the systematic budgeting of time to professional demands—all these traits of our industrial civilization with its factory whistles, its engagement calendar, its balanced bank accounts, would be absent from his world. We can hardly make a picture of Jesus' life and that of his contemporaries that will be too casual for the facts. The demands for food and shelter were easily met or easily ignored. There is no reason to suppose that in his freedom from worry, in his lack of a place to lay his head, in his life of roving, Jesus was much more of a vagabond or gipsy than many another in the land.

There was another pattern which no doubt provided an unconscious substitute for conscious planning. That was the life of the scribes. In spite of the gospel contrasts Jesus was very much one of them. He had, like them, his disciples; like them he was addressed as "Rabbi." He too taught in the synagogues or by the roadside. In little ways, the gospels quite unconsciously reveal the similarity of Jesus' life to theirs—how his advice is sought, how technical questions are asked him, how his blessing is invoked, or how the sick touch the special tassel which he wore in accordance with the Jewish law.

Just how the rabbis subsisted we do not know; perhaps like Jesus partly on gifts from their admirers. Like him too they had a trade to fall back on. On neither side, whether by accident or not, do we hear much of their practicing it. In any case they do not represent

CHAP. VI     *Purpose, Aim and Motive in Jesus*

a special, well-defined clerical order. As for fixed schedules of teaching, a continuous curriculum of instruction, or any tuition fees, Jesus, and probably the rabbis, were innocent of all these things. Still, they both gave much time to what the gospels call teaching. This was their career, this their life. It need not have been systematized or scheduled to provide Jesus with an entirely sufficient outlet for what in our sophisticated age we express in far more self-directing terms.

In spite of the casualness of economic life in Jesus' environment, which may betoken a similar casualness in other respects towards the investment of time, modern writers have hardly considered the possibilities—even the artistic possibilities—of such an unreflective vagabondage as we have suggested. A teleological theology, a practical ethics, and a modern economics of efficiency make casualness seem unthinkable in any really historical Jesus.

The past felt it sufficient to attribute to Jesus the purpose which theology gave him, viz., that of God's sending him to save the world. Providence, as we call it, had a plan for his life. He knew that plan and followed it, with steadfastness in spite of natural shrinking from its unpleasantness, and with clear sight right up to the cross. No mere man could have been so cognizant of what he was about as Jesus was. In the view of older Christian theology the clear and understanding acceptance of the divine program was inevitable in one who knew as no other his Father's will and shared his Father's purpose.

The divine plan of salvation according to this older view was the central and conscious motive in Jesus' earthly life, and for us today, in our very different rôles from his, the recognition of that plan and of its fulfilment in him constitutes the basis for the Christian life purpose.

Recently, however, emphasis has been laid less on the saving career of Jesus than on his teaching and on his own character. As these are regarded as normative for us, we naturally think of them as important in his own purpose. We also wish to come into dynamic association with his undertakings—and for that reason we wish to know his purpose. We expect to find his secret in the intention of his soul, in his aim, ambition, striving. We are not content with the more static appreciation of God and Christ that used to prevail. We hear nowadays of a struggling God and of a program of Jesus. We call him "The Master Builder." The will of God has taken on a new and congenial meaning in modern Protestantism. Its volitional emphasis is most welcome to our thinking. It is a name now for a movement or campaign that God would endorse, and we look naturally to Jesus for a revelation of this

CHAP. VI     *Purpose, Aim and Motive in Jesus*

ambition. That is what we now mean by the revelation of God in Christ—Christ tells us God's plan for the world:

> For other worlds God has other words,
> But for this world the word of God is Christ.

In this creative and purposive conception of God and Christ, old texts get new meaning and favorite passages emerge, like the Johannine

> My father worketh hitherto and I work.
> Other men have labored and ye have entered
> into their labors.

Even "thy kingdom come, thy will be done" is no longer a passive prayer but a summons to coöperative effort with God in the program revealed by Jesus.

Recent scholarly study of the historical Jesus also has been bringing this aspect into the foreground. The eschatological school began by raising the question in an innocent form: Did Jesus believe in the near end of the world? Those who answered in the affirmative had no alternative but to infer that this expectation colored the whole plan and purpose of Jesus. Hence the problem of consistent (*konsequent*) eschatology was not: Must we retain the eschatological sayings in our records? but it was: What was Jesus aiming at in view of the near coming of the kingdom? The extremists like Wrede and Schweitzer differ from the more moderate eschatologists precisely in this, that taking an element which we may admit cannot be excised from the background of Jesus' thought and teaching, which was doubtless part of his *Weltanschauung*, they attempt to explain by it his actions. In other words, they are reducing Jesus to a consistent purpose.

There can be no doubt that the expectation of a near cataclysm always gives the urgency of crisis. Urgency is always suggestive of dominating purpose. Yet even if we accept at its face value that tenseness, that undivided earnestness of Jesus' most rigorous ethic and his most imminent apocalyptic, any corresponding definiteness of direction is not easy to visualize except in quite general terms. Apocalyptic is only too likely to be panicky pressure rather than constructive aim. If Jesus had drive, had he also direction?

The social school of interpreters of Jesus also tend to cast their interpretation into the form of a purpose. They regard him as a social reformer, a propagandist with a program. His program was the Kingdom of God or—to change the figure a little startlingly—the brotherhood of man and the fatherhood of God. His gospel was not merely some academic abstract of a Utopia but a constitution for a better society for which Jesus both lived and died. Like the eschatologists these in-

CHAP. VI  *Purpose, Aim and Motive in Jesus*

terpreters wish to relate Jesus' action to a definite policy or program. They find the key to that program in his social teaching to others. They assume that his own life was shaped by the same purpose—a Purpose with a capital P—unwavering, conscious, absorbing, glorifying.

This way of looking at Jesus has been further reinforced by the political interpretation of him which in America and England has been called forth by the Great War. A series of studies has appeared relating Jesus to the political scene of his day, the parties and their programs. In the light of all these circumstances we are asked what was Jesus' policy for his nation, for its relation to Rome and for international affairs. Surely he was no ignorant or provincial peasant but a "lord of thought," a consummate statesman, in contrast to the fanatical extremists or the time-serving politicians of his day. His background of politics—nationalism, pacifism, and imperialism—is the true key "towards an understanding of Jesus," as Simkhovitch phrases it. What, we may ask, using the title of another book, was "the proposal of Jesus"?[4]

The political understanding of Jesus is, of course, only a special phase of the general modern social interpretation of his life and message. Our recent thinking on our own national and international questions has turned our attention to this special field, with a

## *The Peril of Modernizing Jesus*  CHAP. VI

most anxious desire for "the guidance of Jesus for today" as Cadoux names another book. But we are not so much in search of legislative prescription about loving enemies or giving tribute to Caesar as an older generation would have been. We are concerned rather to detect behind Jesus' life and sayings a regulative purpose that will explain both his own conduct and his advice to others. For example we are told that Jesus devoted himself to averting the disaster of the year 70 A.D. though Jerusalem refused to accept his advice because she "knew not the things that belonged to her peace." But nevertheless Jesus and his words are to be understood like the glorious but ineffective career of Jeremiah that preceded a like catastrophe some six centuries before.

Another aspect of present day scholarly thought about Jesus, associated with these that I have mentioned and like them leading to an emphasis on the element of intention, is our interest in the Messianic self-consciousness of Jesus. Unless we deal very drastically with our records we must admit that Jesus claimed, accepted, or at least did not deny that in some sense he himself was the expected Messiah. It may be doubtful how far he conformed to the conventional rôle of such a figure, but as Messiah the reflection on a special function of his own would be if anything more necessary than if he had classed himself with groups less unique like

CHAP. VI     *Purpose, Aim and Motive in Jesus*

"prophets and wise men and scribes." Without going into this question in detail, we can say that Messiahship, if taken seriously by Jesus or by us, must be thought of almost essentially as an active and aggressive part to be played with a definite objective and a definite program. Whatever we may think of the particular solution Professor Carver proposed, his striking essay on "The Economic Factor in the Messiahship of Jesus"[5] indicates how, even beyond theological circles, many believe that Jesus as the Messiah must have adopted a well-considered program towards a well-recognized goal. The temptation story of Q is perhaps the most satisfactory and extensive proof text of a weighed and reflected Messianic purpose of Jesus.[6]

A favorite device among modern psychoanalysts of Jesus makes Messiahship the result rather than the cause of his life purpose. They would assume for him first an inner urgency, a sense of divine calling and of a duty to be performed. In its scope and in its climax the fatal career of Jesus did not suggest the rôle usually expected of the Messiah. Yet the call was too insistent to be brushed aside, too necessary to be evaded, too certain to be less than divine. Thus in spite of himself Jesus was forced to admit that he was the Messiah. By this hypothesis the plan of his life was not deduced by Jesus from his Messiahship but rather *vice versa*.

*The Peril of Modernizing Jesus*     CHAP. VI

Now all this study of Jesus' Messiahship is to be welcomed. It is a real grappling with historical problems. That "Jesus is the Christ" or better "the Christ is Jesus" was the oldest creed of the church. It was established by the scriptures and it guaranteed the second coming with its blessings. Never since the earliest days has the Messiahship of Jesus (as distinct from his Incarnation, Lordship, Saviorhood and Divinity) entered so largely into Christian thinking as in our own day.

But even when Messiahship is thought of as not accepted by Jesus, as in Professor Case's biography, the element of purpose colors the picture. Two of the chapters in that book "Jesus' Choice of His Task," "Jesus' Pursuit of His Task," show that the biographer is thinking of Jesus as one would of any modern dynamic subject.[7] Jesus is taken for granted as no pawn of destiny but the master of his fate, the captain of his soul. Traditional rôles may be accepted or declined; that makes little difference in the life of one who by hypothesis has proved the most influential factor in history. *Ex nihilo nihil fit.* Problems are solved by those who see them as problems, who have skill to analyze them, and wisdom and insight to settle them.

This and indeed all the tendencies I have spoken of, are due to two most commendable characteristics of our time. One is the return to a fresh study of the con-

CHAP. VI    *Purpose, Aim and Motive in Jesus*

tents of the gospels. The other is the attempt to understand Jesus in the light of reality, particularly of historical reality. Perhaps modern study and emphasis need some correction in the light of what I may call historical psychology. We have tried to understand his political, social, economic and religious environment but have we ever attempted sufficiently to visualize the difference in inner psychology between his day and ours?

Before I attempt to evaluate further this modern interest in the purpose of Jesus I must again say a word about a difficulty that haunts us at every step of historical inquiry—the difficulty of knowing how far we can trust our gospels.

The reader will not be surprised if I advise that for this question we omit entirely the sayings of Jesus in the Fourth Gospel. Whatever elements of historical value that most inscrutable book contains, they are to be found, I think, least of all in its portrayal of Jesus' self-consciousness. Precisely in this matter of Jesus' sense of knowing what he was about, the fourth Evangelist seems to have introduced what Professor Jacks would call "perspective." Jesus in its pages knew not only what he wanted but also what would happen. He was a thoroughly self-conscious, self-directing God. He knew when his hour had or had not come. He "knew what was in man" and he knew God. But,

*The Peril of Modernizing Jesus*       CHAP. VI

above all, he knew what he was about from beginning to end.

How far do the synoptic gospels inject the same alien interpretation into the mind of Jesus, and how far do they guide us aright by providing original and accurate data of his life and words out of which to reconstruct that mind for ourselves? The answer to this question can hardly be unanimous in the present state of opinion. Scarcely a liberal minister exists today who has not publicly implied that he could gauge the intention of Jesus somewhat from these more primitive records. At any rate the data are not so unambiguous that unanimity about Jesus' purpose is easily attained. A questionnaire to theological students, to ministers, even to New Testament scholars would produce a great variety of answers to the question: What was Jesus' purpose?

Certainly the synoptic gospels do not often represent Jesus as discussing his program. They have much less of that kind of Christian interpretation than we find in John. There are certain sentences beginning "I came," followed by a clause of purpose, which may be suspected as Christian interpretation; but on the whole the trouble with the synoptic gospels is their sheer lack of material that would lead to a decision on this subject. Granted the genuineness of the bulk of them we may still conclude that while we know of many

CHAP. VI  *Purpose, Aim and Motive in Jesus*

obiter dicta and anecdotes of Jesus we are not in a position to recover a knowledge of his central purpose.

The "I came" passages are indeed of considerable interest and I pause a moment to review them.[8] Some of them are introduced in the impersonal way "The son of man came." They look a little too reflective or objective for Jesus, but we can hardly believe that this use of "son of man" which the evangelists limit to Jesus' lips never actually came from him.

There are other reasons, however, for regarding these programmatic utterances as secondary. Many of them seem to be intended to answer the reflection of the church, as for example, "Think not that I came."

The principal passages are:

The son of man came not be ministered unto but to minister and to give his life a ransom for many.

I came not to call the righteous but sinners (to repentance).

Think not that I came to destroy the law or the prophets. I came not to destroy but to fulfil.

Think not that I came to cast peace on the earth. I came not to cast peace but a sword. For I came to divide a man, etc.

I came to cast fire on the earth, and what will I if it is already kindled? I have a baptism to be baptized with, and how am I constrained until it is completed. Do you suppose that I came to give peace on the earth? No, I tell you, but division.

*The Peril of Modernizing Jesus*          CHAP. VI

For the son of man came not to destroy men's lives but to save.

I was not sent save unto the lost sheep of the house of Israel.[10]

Of these an authority on Judaism says that no scribe or teacher would thus have referred to himself. They did not cherish a sense of special mission, though they thought well of their vocation. These sentences are not to be understood apart from the Messianic idea. Elijah or Messiah would "come" or would "be sent." By whomsoever they were thus first phrased they would involve Messiahship for Jesus.

A recent student of the synoptic tradition regards these as "the sayings in which the faith of the church in Jesus, in his work, his fate and his person, find their expression." He continues: "The predictions of the passion in Mark 8,31; 9,31; 10,33-34 and others were first created by the church; similarly also either all or most of the sayings which speak of the coming of Jesus, like Matt. 5,17; Mark 10,45. They are expressed from the retrospective standpoint in which an interpretation of the life of Jesus has become possible." [11]

In one or two cases I think we can see the reference to Jesus' mission growing. The most conspicuous example is in the parallels:

CHAP. VI  *Purpose, Aim and Motive in Jesus*

| Mark | Luke |
|---|---|
| Let us go elsewhere into the adjacent towns, in order that I may preach there, for I came out for this purpose. | It is necessary for me to preach the good news of the Kingdom of God also to the other cities, because I was sent for this purpose.[9] |

Here we have Jesus sent from heaven, not merely escaping from Capernaum as probably Mark means to say; and more than that we have Luke's little but effective δεῖ as in other Lucan passages; for instance: "It is necessary for me to be in my Father's house."

Perhaps another warning may be added. It is too easy to arrive at a man's purpose by seeing what he accomplished. We reverently assume that Jesus in particular was a success, that even his death was in accord and not in conflict with his aim. Hence we read back into his mind the results which we see to have followed. But life often works the other way. Men aim at one thing and find another. They build better than they know, or God takes their failures and makes successes of them. We must be ready, if evidence warrants, to assign to Jesus as a purpose something which in no way was actually fulfilled. There is no need for face-saving at this distance. We can recognize that the early Church "supposed that it was he who should redeem Israel," but Paul admitted that in his time Israel was not yet saved, and a later writer testified: "He came to his own and his own received him not."

In fact the whole notion of success is bound up with the very conception that I wish to challenge—purpose. If lives are read in terms of purpose then accomplishment is their measure. But suppose we could eliminate purpose. Then there would be no need to pass the judgment of success or failure.

Let us turn then to consider, from the standpoint of his ethical teaching, what we may say about the purpose of Jesus. I say from the standpoint of his *ethical* teaching because I believe we know more on this than on any other phase of him—both in bulk and in reliability. Jesus' words on conduct and character are a more stable basis than our information on his own religious and moral life or on his religious advice to others.

Our view of Jesus' ethical teaching depends, as does every other question, on what we think was Jesus' purpose. Jesus' main purpose may have been to instil a new way of life, by his teaching and example to establish as far as possible in contemporary Judaism, or in the leavening group within it which his followers so imperfectly became, a higher standard of conduct. If he expected the near end of the world or if he hoped to establish through his teaching this better order, whether as teacher or as herald, he may have de-

CHAP. VI  *Purpose, Aim and Motive in Jesus*

liberately worked out and consistently applied a new, complete standard of ethics.

If he aimed to build a church, this is again not inconsistent. His church could have been intended to embody these principles. No matter how religious Jesus' outlook was he may have been greatly interested in the fruits of religion. Jesus' purpose is often expressed in such terms as Messiah, or even more generally as doing the will of God. But all such definitions are extremely vague in themselves and most Christians assume that Jesus had one controlling guiding purpose in his life and that, even if circumstances caused him to change his method, he was deliberately working out a plan that consciously included the betterment of society or at least of his generation in Galilee and Jerusalem along lines of an ethical and social as well as a spiritual nature.

The modern age, even without reference to the gospels, tends to believe that Jesus must so have lived. Every good man is expected now to have such a unity, definiteness and consciousness of purpose. Even if we cannot discover it we assume it in Jesus, and mostly we can read such unity, definiteness and consciousness of purpose into the gospel story.

We assume very often, further, that Jesus' purpose was based on a knowledge of the factors involved. If he was dealing with the nation he must have studied the national situation and its present standards and policies, and he must have determined some program, which, beginning with the status quo in the church, the state or the empire, would mould it more nearly to the heart's desire. If Jesus was dealing with individuals we assume for him the same kind of diagnosis—a profound knowledge of human needs, impulses, aspirations and capacities, and we attempt to discover in him a technique of personal and collective evangelism based upon sound psychological and pedagogical principles.

I am doubtful whether we do not read into Jesus' life more of a campaign than existed. The followers of Jesus and his biographers did this in their picture of his sending out missionaries, but were they right? Economic life in Jesus' day was simple; was his personal program not also hand to mouth? Suppose we try to picture a typical day in Jesus' life. It was not lived by schedule probably; his social contacts like those of Socrates were of the most accidental sort. He was neither a systematic teacher of his disciples, nor careful in his evangelistic planning. He wandered hither and thither in Galilee. He sowed his seed largely at random and left results to God. More depended, he believed, on the soil, than on the sowing. Probably much that is commonly said about the general purpose of Jesus' life and the specific place in that pur-

CHAP. VI     *Purpose, Aim and Motive in Jesus*

pose of detailed incidents is modern superimposition upon a nearly patternless life and upon nearly patternless records of it.

What I wish to propose is that Jesus probably had no definite, unified, conscious purpose, that an absence of such a program is *a priori* likely and that it suits well the historical evidence. Further I think that this explains some of the phenomena connected with his teaching.

The sense of purpose, objective, etc., as necessary for every good life is more modern than we commonly imagine. Some men in antiquity lived under it—a sense of calling, mission, etc. Paul may be an example, though we should recall that the Greek omits the word "do" in the familiar sentence of his, "This one thing I *do*." My impression is that Jesus was largely casual. He reacted to situations as they arose but probably he had hardly a program or plan. His martyrdom is not in conflict with such a view, for one form of martyrdom at least is that of men who, without planning or scheming, submit to adversity as it comes. The religious man in particular leaves planning to God and simply submits to the inevitable. He may foresee it, but that is not the same as courting it or planning it or incorporating it into his self-justification. As Jesus says, "I go on my way today and tomorrow and the third day I am perfected." A large part of Jesus' say-

*The Peril of Modernizing Jesus*      CHAP. VI

ings, interpreted as indicating an intelligent and chosen aim, may be understood in this sense of passive fatalism. Submission to the will of God does indeed give life a kind of unity, yet it lacks all that creative planning, intelligent selection, singleness of purpose and the like that we usually mean in our efforts to preach the integration of life.

There is nothing irreverent or improbable in such a view of Jesus. Modern purposiveness has no guarantee of divinity about it, though we naturally attribute it to God and to Jesus, making them in our own image. Perhaps modern lives if analyzed would prove to be quite casual, varied and ununified in spite of the formula of integration which a self-conscious age demands that respectable men adopt for themselves. St. Francis is really not the last saint whose virtue was spontaneous and unpremeditated. Organization rapidly followed his movement as it follows many saints and prophets, but it is usually a by-product more than an original aim. If we may judge Jesus by the characteristics of mankind in general he is likely to have lived much by custom and by uncoordinated impulse and to have made conscious decisions only of a rather isolated and varied character, and the more we regard him a genius in any lines the more likely it is that in those lines he was dependent on flashes of insight and

CHAP. VI  *Purpose, Aim and Motive in Jesus*

inspiration rather than upon some conscious planning and labored artistry.

If Jesus was in this respect a child of his age, this explains some things in his social teaching. Our records suggest that Jesus had much to say about conduct. But they suggest further:

1. His remarks were usually in answer to concrete cases or questions.

2. The motives he appealed to are extraordinarily varied and show no derivation from a fixed standard but rather, as with most opinions of moral questions, a mixture of reasons. Sometimes he appealed to prudence; sometimes he simply gave advice as axiomatic, or assigned a conventional reason. Noteworthy for their absence (at least in the record) are some of the all-controlling purposes of ethics, like altruism, value of personality, greatest good to the greatest number, brotherhood. We may and often do read between the lines some of them but we should remember that we are not reading the gospels.

We need not suppose that this variety of motive was merely accommodation to the varied needs and points of appeal in Jesus' hearers. It perhaps correctly reflects the mixed character of Jesus' own bases of conduct and judgment.

With this view accord the apparent statements of

his own purpose—already mentioned: "I came not to send peace but division," "I came to cast fire on the earth," "I came not to call the righteous but sinners to repentance," "I was not sent except to the lost sheep of the house of Israel," "The son of man came to seek and to save the lost." All these, if genuine, are simply the varying ways of expressing his reaction to successive incidents or situations. Such unity of purpose as we can give his life is our own reading of it in the light of the records. Very early Christians summed up the meaning of Jesus' life (and especially his death) in terms he would never have recognized:

To give life and to give it more abundantly.
He became a curse to redeem us from under a curse.
For the joy that was set before him he endured the cross.
Being in the form of God—he emptied himself.
For your sakes he became poor.
To this end was I born and to this end came I into the world that I might bear witness to the truth.
I am the way, the truth and the life.
To give his life a ransom for many.[12]

With this accords also the lack of a satisfactory summary in the gospels of any principle for general application. We ask for Jesus' advice in a nutshell and we are referred to the Sermon on the Mount, or more briefly the Golden Rule, or the two great commands.

CHAP. VI  *Purpose, Aim and Motive in Jesus*

Other more modern terms for unifying Jesus' teaching are love, service, the value of the individual, the fatherhood of God and the brotherhood of man.

All these may be useful rubrics for modern Christian ideals but there is grave doubt whether Jesus had any such conscious unifying principle, or even whether his attitudes allow themselves to be reduced to one such modern key explanation. Several of these headings do not gain any considerable support from the gospel materials. Others have at least the character of being probable since they are natural for any Jew, but at the same time they are not original or unique. Both the Golden Rule and the choice of the two commandments to love God and man were perhaps current Jewish summaries. They are traceable to Hillel and Akiba respectively, while one of the commandments, to love the Lord thy God, has the central authority, the familiarity and the prestige of the daily Jewish creed called the Shema. In both cases Jesus says of his summary, not "Here is the gospel" or "the New Testament," but, "This is (or on this hangs) the law and the prophets." Would it not be simpler to say that the aim of Jesus was to live according to the will of God, of which the law with the prophets formed the chief revelation?

This leads us back to the knotty problem of Jesus' relationship to Judaism. In spite of all ingenious efforts no one formula brings into harmony all the utterances of Jesus on this subject. Now he is apparently rejecting, now insisting on, Jewish ethics. Now he apparently accepts the Old Testament law, while rejecting the oral tradition based upon it. Now he quotes one passage against another. Now he accepts the Jews' religion but criticizes their leaders. Now he distinguishes between the teaching and the doing of the Pharisees. He says their righteousness is too meticulous or too formal or too much for display or too hypocritical or not righteous enough.

The modern mind tries to get out of all this a single definitive formula that will explain everything. One easily assumes that if Jesus had a controlling purpose, and that if that purpose included giving social teaching, Jesus probably had a definite code or principle. This code most naturally would be defined in terms of contemporary Judaism, and hence our next inquiry is for some formula that will place Jesus' teaching in connection with that of his age.

Now, after all, few of us can be reduced in our views of social duty to a formula in terms of some code of contemporary ethics. We share it here, we disagree there, we side with one contemporary party or the other. Probably the same was true of Jesus. To a very large extent his viewpoint was ordinary Judaism. He endorsed the ten commandments and probably be-

CHAP. VI     *Purpose, Aim and Motive in Jesus*

lieved in the law (when correctly understood) as the revealed will of God. He argues that certain things are as bad as what the law prohibited. Study of contemporary teaching shows that Jesus agrees in many of the more striking and beautiful parts of his social teaching with the standards of the rabbis. Judaism was a principal source of his judgment. In the main, he reiterates with insistence what others have taught or what may be counted on to be recognized by his hearers as right. He rarely seems to be propounding something new. When he criticizes a contemporary standard he is usually agreeing with some other contemporary standard. Some questions were simply moot questions of his day—divorce, great commandment, tribute, capital punishment for adultery. Jesus sometimes takes sides, sometimes evades the issue.

Neither in a unifying principle nor in detail does Jesus betray an independent and harmonious codification of his own, but a series of judgments—many old, perhaps a few new, many sound according to our own estimate. In all this he behaves just as one would expect of a pure, earnest, pious Jew of Galilee in the reign of Tiberius.

In denying to Jesus much of the modern formulation of purpose we must beware of two extremes of negation. First, though Jesus did not share our characteristically modern emphasis upon a conscious life purpose, neither did he definitely reject it. It was not presented to him as an alternative ideal to his own rather passive and casual career. Thoreau, for example, who most of all moderns agrees with this trait in Jesus, yet differs decidedly just because he is in revolt against a modern standard. If any of us today rebel against our inherited Puritan traditions of obedience to active duty, of labor and accomplishment, and allow ourselves to drift indifferent to the usual watchwords of "life with a purpose," "integrating our personalities," "forging out our careers," "God has a plan for every life," it will be more like Thoreau's protest than like the naïve fatalism and spontaneousness of Jesus. We can quote Jesus only in part for our attitude, for the modern scene about us will never leave such an unmodern and unambitious ambition unchallenged.

Second, the life of Jesus is not to be regarded as wholly without unity even if it lacked the modern type of conscious planning. For the true quality of life is not in the conscious, but in the subconscious, not in pose and profession but in deed and in truth. The native intuition of Jesus gave him no doubt a deep-lying consistency, what Thomas à Kempis would call an interior simplicity.[18] Whatever he said and did was not brought by him into accord with some external criterion; it sprang from an inner coördination of life. In such cases logical consistency is not always present,

CHAP. VI *Purpose, Aim and Motive in Jesus*

and is not intended; but a moral consistency may be there, an habitual reaction and a natural self-accord. There is perhaps no better description of Jesus' career than those phrases in the book of Acts which describe its spontaneous consistency and casualness. It was "all the days that he went in and out among us," say the apostles, or "he went about doing good." Such a life gets its unity neither from its goal nor from any standard of action but from an unphrased inner quality and temperament. Perhaps some day in the future historical students of the gospels will realize that there is more profit in inquiring into these hidden habits of his soul than in attempting to fit the anecdotes and sayings of Jesus into a program of his life. These hidden habits rather than the latter give us a sense of unison between him and ourselves.

If Jesus was not self-conscious about his program he may not have been conscious about his motives either. In spite of our own interest in the subject and in spite of the fact that ethical teachers even in his own time distinguished motives behind apparently identical actions, I find little evidence in the gospels that Jesus made that distinction. Is it their motive that makes him call the Pharisees hypocrites? He does condemn prayer, almsgiving and fasting that is done "to be seen of men." But as we have already seen, he appeals more often than not to what modern ethics would have to call a "self-regarding" motive.

Of the motives of his own action we must admit that we are left to the veriest conjecture. It is interesting—in the light of conventional talk about Christianity—that Jesus nowhere in the synoptic gospels uses "love" of either his own or his Father's attitude to men.[14] Shall we say that when Jesus saw the multitudes of misguided and unvirtuous lives threatened with a near day of judgment the prevailing feeling was pity and fear? Or did the ideals of life that he cherished so press themselves forward from within him that whenever he was asked advice or was confronted with opposite examples he could not choose but speak? To our embarrassment as professed altruists we discovered that Jesus appeals to the self-regard of men for their own welfare. Was Jesus himself so impelled? Was he looking out for number one? Did he lose his life to save it, deny himself to gain a hundredfold, take up the cross to gain a world?

But even the motives he appeals to in others may not really represent a reasoned conclusion about the springs of action. To the strong statement made above that he appealed generally to self-interest and rarely to altruism many will object that we are judging merely by what he is quoted as saying. Perhaps he left some important considerations unsaid. Perhaps he took for

CHAP. VI    *Purpose, Aim and Motive in Jesus*

granted that his hearers accepted unselfishness as proper conduct and he merely wished to reinforce it by pointing out what was less obvious—its advantageous results to the one who practices it. If so, we must at least say that he took for granted what we are wont to argue and argued what we are wont to take for granted.

But in spite of his argument, on what did Jesus really count as likely to induce people to accept his advice? How could Jesus expect a man to sell all he had and follow him, or to rejoice in persecution, or to forgive his debtors, or to choose the humblest places at feasts? This is a question I have often asked myself and as often have wondered whether possibly he never really thought the matter through. In that case we can infer little from silence. He does not, for example, press his personal claims as a ground for heeding him, but the lack of appeal to his own authority is no evidence that he was modest or silent about his Messianic rôle. Possibly he counted on the self-evident rightness of his standards of conduct, so that when he suggested a course of action its intrinsic appeal would meet a response in other men's hearts and they would follow. Surely this is the most potent force on which the exponent of ideals can depend—the axiomatic correctness of his advice and the *noblesse oblige* of his hearers. But again we can hardly be sure that he figured it out that way. Or again did experience teach him, had he learned by trial and error, the pedagogic values of different appeals? Very likely he had not. Probably Jesus and even Paul would have been horrified at the suggestion that his converting of men was due to some skilful plan of his own devising. Consideration of a technique would be quite foreign to the whole thinking of such lives. Then neither subjective self-analysis nor objective testing of methods belongs to the mentality of Jesus. Neither internal resolve nor external circumstance tended to conscious planning in a mind like his.

In such questions we reach the area of utmost psychological obscurity in any life—much more in a life so little known and so far away. But even if there was much more self-analysis in Jesus than I have supposed, much more consciousness of life issues, of his own standing and what others thought of him, I would still remind us that it could easily have taken many other forms than the kind that first occurs to us, viz., the formulating of a plan, the study of method and the adjustment of one's conduct to that means and end.

Self-consciousness need not take the forms of planned purpose and tested results. Another fertile outlet for introspective judgments is provided by religion. Because we today, rationalist and problem-minded as we

CHAP. VI    *Purpose, Aim and Motive in Jesus*

are, relate the two we need not suppose that Jesus would do so. On the contrary, religion in his time and circle considered, much more than one's own plans, God's will. Obedience to God's will or being well pleasing in his sight, far more than accomplishment of a purpose, was the criterion of success or basis for self-satisfaction. The ancient equivalent of much modern calculation, purpose, and self-analysis was religion. It is appropriate, therefore, that our next and concluding chapter should deal with the religion of Jesus.

Chapter VII

# THE RELIGION OF JESUS

WITH that ease with which he seemed always to be able to analyze history, Professor Harnack once struck off the distinction—the gospel of Jesus and the gospel about Jesus. All study of our sources makes us realize that there is no small difference between them. The same is true if we use the terms—the religion of Jesus and the religion about Jesus. The religion of Jesus is now to be the subject of our consideration.

In our own time as never before this subject has seemed important, not only historically but practically. An earlier generation was content nearly to ignore the actual religion of Jesus himself. Either the message which he preached or that of which he was the central theme seemed far more important than his own experience. He was little considered to be an example for our religion. Of course in so far as he was divine, or even unique among men, he was not so much to be imitated as to be worshipped or obeyed.[1] In so far as he was human his value was his ethical precept and prac-

CHAP. VII  *The Religion of Jesus*

tice. So neither conservative nor liberal theology paid in the past much attention to Jesus' own religion.

There is much evidence that in the present time a new emphasis is being placed on the religious experience of Jesus and the reasons for such a change are not hard to find. Such books as Bundy's *The Religion of Jesus* and G. W. Fiske's *Jesus' Own Religion* are probably symptomatic of a new and growing trend in America to regard as important Jesus' religious experience.

In part this new emphasis is due to a new place which religious experience holds in the moden thought of religion. Our scientific training has made us aim at actual empirical bases for religion. The older reliance on belief which some time ago gave place to a reliance on conduct has now been further replaced by a reliance on experience. Neither faith nor works can save you, but something which comes to you, which is the expression of your inner life, or rather is the expression in your inner life of the divine. No doubt the best religious experience is conditioned by the best of belief and practice. No doubt also the best religious experience issues as result in the best of belief and practice. But for several modern forms of Christianity the central validating element is experience. Naturally, therefore, we point to that aspect in the life of Jesus, lying as it does behind his deeds and his words.

*The Peril of Modernizing Jesus*       CHAP. VII

But hand in hand with the new interest in religious experience has gone a change in our confidence in old standards. The story of the quest for a valid external guide has constantly run parallel to the quest of the historical Jesus. They are equally fascinating chapters in the evolution of modern thought. Human nature, incurably desirous of some objective standards, has repeatedly sought such standards in the church or in the Bible. An authoritative church was replaced in the Reformation by an authoritative book. Since the Reformation Protestants have been trying to discover within that book the authoritative element. The Old Testament became less authoritative than the New and within the New Testament Paul less than Jesus. At the same time the standard of a creed or of a plan of salvation in which Jesus played a prominent rôle was found to be not only less congenial but less Biblical than the authority of Jesus' own person. Even in this area the demand for authority has continued its recessive tendency. From the universal authority of Jesus as infallible and unique, modern thinking compelled a retreat to the ethical teaching. Here was the field in which Jesus was a genius. Since, however, literary study of the gospels made it clear that the sayings they preserved were neither complete nor absolutely accurate, a more recent tendency has been to erect as a standard Jesus' own character. But if we can be only imperfectly informed

CHAP. VII  *The Religion of Jesus*

even on this, and if furthermore that character was the outcome of a religious personality and experience, we naturally make one further retreat and expect to find our standard in the religion of Jesus.

While thus assuming the normative character of Jesus' religion men are as likely as in any other field that we have discussed to indulge in excessive modernization. From what has gone before our problem is obvious. We ask ourselves: What can we safely infer from our records of Jesus' own experience? What does contemporary Judaism suggest as the sort of religion natural for a first century Jew?[2] Can we indicate where Jesus fitted in this circle of religious life and where his own religion had a special or unusual, if not unique, character? And, finally, what ideals of modern religion are we most likely to inject falsely into the historical setting?

At once the question arises: How far may we infer the religion of Jesus from what is implicit in his teachings, or must we distinguish his own religion not only from what has been taught in his name, but even from his own teaching? Every teacher's words tend to correspond to his own experience, and it is natural and just to infer that for Jesus himself religion was very much what he assumed it should be for others. That would be true of a modern preacher unless he was consciously a hypocrite or was trying by a pedagogic

*The Peril of Modernizing Jesus*  CHAP. VII

method to lead others to goals which he had attained through other means. A modern preacher, too, does not hesitate (with adequate safeguards to his modesty) to promulgate a religious ideal which he has not yet attained, or to draw from the classical or contemporary experience of others illustrations and standards for his hearers.

I cannot help thinking that religious expression varies much farther than this from the speaker's personal religion. He often regards his hearers' problems as quite different from his own. The things in which they most differ from him he often most strives to overcome and correct, and it is not always easy for him here to apply his own experience. Things which come to him naturally he seeks deliberately to bring to others by whatever means appear to him most likely to succeed in their case. The reasons he gives for his advice are rarely those which have determined his own position. They are often subsequent rationalizations. He may practice what he preaches, but not for the same reasons. In this he is neither insincere nor even conscious. His preaching, for example, is far more influenced by conventional or traditional standards than by his religious life. Much in the latter is controlled by personal temperament or outward circumstances rather than adapted to the needs of his hearers. What is true of others in this regard seems likely in the case of Jesus

## The Religion of Jesus

to a high degree. If we are right in supposing that to him a sense of value seemed self-evident and that his religious ideas were fundamental and largely subconscious, in so far as he gives reasons or makes religion articulate, his teaching differs from his own religion. We may well ask of each argument of Jesus, did it seem that way to him? Did he forgive others because God forgave him? Did he refrain from judging others that he might not be judged? Was it because he wished others to do the same to him that he treated men as he did? Did he humble himself that he might be exalted? Did God's care for the birds and flowers really free Jesus from anxiety? And did the two commandments which he quoted really form the foundation of his own love for God and for men?

Although these are legitimate questions, I ask them not to answer them but to show how difficult they are to answer. The natural assumption that Jesus' teaching perfectly reflects his own experience needs some reservation. There was something in the forefront of his teaching that was not conspicuous in his experience. Conversely there was something merely implied in his teaching that was decisive in his experience. Once Jesus is represented as referring his hearers to what they of themselves think to be right. Such unmeasured, independent, axiomatic impulses were probably often the real determinants of his own life.

In spite of this warning it is tempting and, within limits, legitimate to use Jesus' teaching as indicative of his experience. What he says must at least accord with his experience, though the reasons he gives are sometimes the proofs rather than the causes of his viewpoint. Probably he did not stress his own authority as the ground for accepting his advice, and the synoptic gospels scarcely represent him as doing so. Rather he expected those who heard him to arrive at the same conclusions as he did for the same reasons, by the same process, out of the same background. His use of parable and illustration is therefore striking. If we may infer at all from the way he taught, he believed that moral and religious truths were illustrated and confirmed by the analogies of our ordinary life. As seed varies in initial character, some of it being wheat and some tares, as each plant whether fig tree or thistle produces fruit of its own kind, as the same seed produces more or less fruitfully depending on its soil—so it is with the character of men. Or, to take some illustrations from human life, as the lost sheep receives more attention than the secure ones, as faithful servants are rewarded more surely than the faithless ones, as persistence, foresight and humility are commendable in human dealings—so it is in our relation with God.

In other words Jesus, as we should expect, regarded the religious relation as analogous to the natural and

## The Religion of Jesus

the human. We have already affirmed that Jesus believed in a personal deity: so did his contemporaries and so have most religious persons except the most scientifically or metaphysically minded. You may call his view anthropomorphic but that adjective should not arouse surprise or censure. He also believed that God was in and behind nature. You may find in the dictionary a long adjective for that, which smacks of some historical heresies, but that should not bother you either. For our present subject the important outcome of these aspects of God is that it makes him akin to man and to man's experience in the world. For Jesus religion is an area continuous with the rest of our life. Analogous principles prevail, similar phenomena are to be expected. Because life is all of one piece religion is far less supernatural and superhuman to Jesus than to much of our own thinking. Or, if one prefers to put it so, nature and humanity are far more divine to him than to us. There is a significance not easily explored to its limits in this conjunct character of Jesus' world. He made no dividing line, no conscious transfer from one area to another, when he illustrated the Kingdom of God by parables in the realm of nature or of human life. Some have suggested that he used the method of parable with others because he himself discovered religious truth in that way. Such may well be the case, but if it is, it only confirms what we have been saying of the homogeneity of life as it appeared to him with his theistic assumptions concerning nature and history and his anthropomorphic views about God.[3]

The question we have been discussing of the relation between Jesus' teaching and his experience, though of interest, has in reality but little practical bearing upon the topic of his specifically religious experience. Religious experience as that term is commonly used today is not a major subject of his teaching. He has in our surviving records very little to tell men of their relation to God in any interior and subjective sense. We might like to find in him some instruction about religious life as an inner commerce with the divine, but we are face to face with teaching that is much more objective and external in its viewpoint. The thing which Jesus' words seem to demand is not a consciousness of divine approval so much as a consciousness of being worthy of such approval. Our thought of God, of his demands and his promises, is the sanction for Jesus' advice about conduct, and this thought is not something categorical and axiomatic as though a pure inward revelation but is a commonplace of both Jesus and his contemporaries which can be illustrated and confirmed by quite objective illustrations. Instead of arguing against worry by appeal to experience of inner peace, he appeals to the more objective and rational consideration of the clothing of the lilies and the feeding of the birds. Prayer is

CHAP. VII  *The Religion of Jesus*

justified by outward effects. Even when the prayer, fasting, and almsgiving of the hypocrites are condemned for very externality, we are not reminded of any richer religious experience on the part of the less ostentatious. We merely imply that the experience is richer because for us it would be so. When we are told that the publican went down from temple prayer more justified than the Pharisee our modern minds read into the contrast a presumption of deeper inner satisfaction and spiritual reality. "Justified" for the evangelist very likely means what it sometimes means to Paul—something external, forensic. The widespread modern feeling that religion in Paul is a matter of status while for Jesus it is a matter of experience is not only unfair to Paul: it is largely inaccurate for Jesus. Jesus, too, like his great follower, shares the Jewish idea of religion as a man's standing before God, as an obedience to God's will, and as a destiny to be determined between us. It is not for Jesus exactly a legal status, but it is nevertheless external, objective, practical. Paul with his self-analysis and emotional loyalty, with his Christ-mysticism and sense of being controlled and possessed, approaches much more nearly to the modern man's idea of religious experience.

The trouble may of course be in the scantiness of our gospel records, but we are speaking now of Jesus' recorded teaching and we have no right to add at will to

*The Peril of Modernizing Jesus* CHAP. VII

it. How little does Jesus have to say of the devotional life. He does indeed teach about prayer but it is prayer as an exercise rather than as a self-expression, as a practical expedient rather than an experience. Fasting and almsgiving are associated with it in the Sermon on the Mount as they were among the Jews. As to what Jesus thought of them, most of us have quite definite opinions, based largely on our own attitude. They seem to us far more external than prayer, and fruits rather than methods of religious devotion. Almsgiving we estimate almost entirely as a social service.

Were I to attempt to explain how the ancient Jews and probably Jesus regarded them I should have to relate them to the fundamental idea of Judaism—the will of God. What seems to us natural, spontaneous, and reasonable seemed to them, because only so could it have sanction, as required obedience to a divine will. No doubt it could be just as willing, natural and satisfying. But religious life can never be quite alike under two such different systems. To many of us personal religion would seem spoiled if it were required, unnatural if prescribed, self-defeating if performed with the clear expectation of reward. These are not the only matters in which we do not readily understand, still less accept, the mentality of Jesus and his contemporaries. We distinguish between Jesus and his contemporaries at just this point. There are passages which

CHAP. VII  *The Religion of Jesus*

give us an excuse for doing so. His attitude to the law and his criticism of its meticulous observance we interpret in much this way, as though Jesus were substituting inner reality for outward form, the spirit for the letter, and experience for expression.

Nowhere earlier have these chapters dealt at length with Jesus' real criticism of Judaism. His agreement with it has been far more conspicuous than his difference. Nor does the topic need now any exhaustive treatment. It is historically a difficult subject in which our records, we may suspect, were subject to disturbing influences of early Christian controversy. Some conflict between Jesus and the Jewish leaders seems historically attested. The cross, though it is a Roman instrument of punishment, is probably witness of some Jewish antagonism. The conflict was more likely to be in the area of Jewish practice than in the area of Jewish belief (including Messianism) or Jewish politics (including Messianism again here).

Granting it to be a fact that Jesus stood definitely opposed to the standards of Pharisaic Judaism, how may we define the exact grounds of difference between them? Such conflicts, when we can study them in better-known religious history, are rarely quite simple, and any too simple formulation comes at once under suspicion. Analogy of like conflicts teaches us further that adherents of the *status quo* usually perceive the

*The Peril of Modernizing Jesus*     CHAP. VII

conflict more promptly, and act more vigorously, than the dissentient minority or protesting reformer. Finally any formulation of Jesus' conflict with Judaism, which, with the excuse of expressing what was then latent or incomplete actually in the light of historical outcome, expresses the contrast in exclusively modern categories, can hardly be true to the conscious mind of Christ. It is another confession of our difficulty in imagining other varieties of religious experience.

Jesus' contrast with Judaism is a natural step to take in any study of his religion. This, the reader may well feel, should have been done at the beginning without any apology or preface. The founder of a new religion largely derived from the old might be expected to show precisely the distinctive elements of his own religious experience in his critique of Judaism. Here we might well expect from our records a full and decisive answer. This historically was the determining item in his career; his biographers cannot have been ignorant of its importance. The answer to this central, simple historical question must surely be forthcoming. What do the scholars of the New Testament tell us?

Such impatient challenges by the layman are familiar to every New Testament scholar. He may give the usual traditional answer, or he may try to be discriminating. In the latter case his reply is usually quite unsatisfactory or even disconcerting.

CHAP. VII　　　　　　　*The Religion of Jesus*

As a discriminating beginning let us take the judgment of Klausner about sabbath healing. No cause of friction is more frequently mentioned in the older gospels than Jesus' cures on the sabbath. This was probably not a major issue in the early church and therefore the gospels may be trusted in referring it back to Jesus. Klausner is a scholar whose judgment at least here may be trusted. What is his reply? It is this. Judaism taught that the sabbath must be observed so strictly that neither patients nor doctors may have medical dealings on that day, unless the disease were dangerous. This then is Klausner's answer. As a ruler of the synagogue said to the congregation who had witnessed Jesus' cure of a chronic patient, "There are six days in the week in which men ought to work: in them therefore come and be healed and not on the day of the sabbath." But Jesus, using the analogy of the care or rescue of farm animals practiced on the sabbath day, sanctioned and practiced in that day the healing of diseases that were not dangerous.[4] That Jesus ignored or abolished the sabbath wholesale we have no evidence. Here then is a dividing line between him and the Pharisees—the line between chronic and acute diseases. In this matter he was certainly more lenient, more humane—we should say, more reasonable. His position on this matter is some clue to his view of the whole, but it is hardly decisive.

*The Peril of Modernizing Jesus*  CHAP. VII

Of Jesus' ultimate view of the Jewish law, two things may be said in this connection. The first is that the problem did not present itself to him in the abstract but in the concrete. He did not work out from an independent principle to its practical application. He worked rather from the individual cases which came to his attention; he formed a judgment on these alone. The more seriously wrong certain forms of law observance seemed to him the more they led him to assert his alternative judgment. Friction and debate with the authorities led him to make on these points assertions which implicitly undermined or weakened the stricter Jewish law as expressed in the Pentateuch or as elaborated in scribal tradition and Pharisaic practice. All this took place without leading Jesus to any wholesale condemnation of the law. If that followed at all, it followed later. What is most important to observe is that the process for him was, to judge by modern analogies, not an application of an inner, prior principle to outward experiences of conflict, but the groping from his instinctive reaction against definite abuses of legalism and legalists to a more spiritual and satisfactory foundation. As between the two factors of inner theory and outer detailed points of revolt, the latter were far more influential in shaping Jesus' position. One feels that the gospels are right in putting at the close of controversial

## The Religion of Jesus

incidents such generalizations as: "The sabbath is made for man, not man for the sabbath." "Whatsoever from without goeth into the man cannot defile him.... That which proceedeth out of the man that defileth the man." They were for Jesus or the early church results or general deductions from opinions formed in definite cases.

In the second place Jesus could remain unweakened in his loyalty to Judaism, his acceptance of the authority of the law and of its teachers, which he in his past life like his present associates accepted, and yet assert what today we should call the prophetic standards of religion—justice and mercy and the love of God. The contrast between the formal and the spiritual was not present to his consciousness, nor at variance within his own character. The two sides of religion have often been retained without any sense of distraction or inconsistency. Spiritual reformers do not intend to overthrow the existing standards; they are not aware that their ideas have that logical outcome. Jewish prophecy really did not break with ceremonial religion whether consuetudinary or codified. The law was influenced by prophecy and prophecy accepted the law. And in Judaism itself contemporary with Jesus both elements plainly co-existed. Modern study and discovery have enriched our knowledge of the varieties of religion within post-Maccabean Judaism, and in all these varieties the law is common and central in spite of special and quite tangential emphases.

There is for example Philo the contemporary of Jesus. His Judaism seems at first sight purely philosophical and ethical, and that with a philosophy and ethics intrinsically Greek in nature and background. Even when (as always) he uses the text of the Pentateuch as the basis of his Hellenistic doctrine he seems to be ignoring its literal meaning, both historical and ceremonial. But this is probably not the case, and for all his allegory Philo almost certainly accepted quite literally the narrative of events and the prescription of duties which the law contained. He at least found it possible to respect and obey the law while holding to a metaphysic and ethic which really and literally were completely independent of it.

In like manner the apocalyptic writers of Judaism maintained a double focus. Though their interest in the end of things is by no means inherently exclusive of law-keeping, it is certainly a quite different kind of interest. It looks to the future rather than the past and its incentive is hope rather than obedience. Scholars speak of this interest as in contrast with first century Pharisaism and there is some evidence that at least later the rabbis looked askance upon the dreamers and schemers of an apocalyptic future. Occasionally Jesus

CHAP. VII  *The Religion of Jesus*

himself seems to ally himself with the critics, but more often with the exponents of a cataclysmic cosmic program. The believers felt themselves good Jews, were loyal to the Jewish law, and had no difficulty in combining the two viewpoints.

Another group—in some respect less well known, but in other ways a more distinct sect—was the Zadokites of Damascus. The long and interesting document discovered in modern times reveals them as most earnest and zealous adherents of the law. Doubtless they did not hold or keep all the Pharisaic traditions and would seem to Caiaphas or Gamaliel heretical and disloyal. Certainly they held definitely unorthodox opinions. From their own point of view they were not thereby surrendering the Torah and its righteousness. They might well have claimed to exceed the righteousness of the scribes and Pharisees.[5]

These groups, all nearly contemporary with Jesus, and others like the Essenes, the later zealots, and the shortlived movement centering around John the Baptist all show how possible and probable it is that Jesus' disloyalty to the Pharisaic standards, for so others considered it, seemed to himself rather the highest loyalty. The areas in which each of these moved had more than one focus, and while in part they came far from overlapping each other, yet the law was for each of them at least one focus and made one common bond between them all. Whether logical or not, such combinations are psychologically possible and not uncommon in religious history. In predicating for Jesus such an unresolved combination we are claiming for him nothing that is different from what we should claim for his predecessors, the prophets, and for his contemporaries, the rabbis. Even the latter believed in both the prophets and the law, in both ethics and ritual. Montefiore may be right in saying that the difference between Jesus and the prophets was in the different conditions under which he spoke:

> When Amos and Hosea and Isaiah spoke, there was no universally recognized Divine and Mosaic Law. When Jesus spoke, there was. Hosea said, in God's name, "I desire loving kindness and not sacrifices." There was no possible retort—"But in the Law of God, which you, like everybody else, acknowledge to be perfect, immutable and divine, sacrifices are required in large numbers." . . . Jesus takes up the prophetic message under conditions which did not exist when the greatest of the Prophets declaimed their most specifically prophetic doctrine. The conflict—both the inward and the outward conflict—was therefore almost inevitable.[6]

As already suggested, the outer conflict was determinative. To this new environment the old prophetic spirit of Jesus reacted. This new environment created in a sense the problem of the law. Jesus and his oppo-

CHAP. VII  *The Religion of Jesus*

nents were not quite in exact opposition. They knew they were defending the law, but Jesus hardly knew he was attacking it.

Such situations often arise in history. Something much the same characterized the early Quakers' attitude to the Bible. They sought to return to primitive Christianity. They wished to live in the same spirit as produced the scriptures. They criticized much in the Christianity around them but they had no thought of condemning the Bible or of setting up the Light within as a separate or superior standard. To their opponents the situation appeared quite otherwise. The contemporary Protestantism not only regarded the Bible as sacred but associated with its sacredness much of their own belief and practice. The Quaker attack on their churches, or sacraments, or ministry, or tithes, or saints' days seemed tantamount to attacking the Bible, while the independent teaching of the Quakers, no matter how much the Bible itself was quoted in their support, seemed the arrogant and blasphemous assertion of individual opinion. The Quakers denied any conflict or contradiction but they left an unresolved problem to trouble their followers in later generations. On the other hand at various times individuals were driven almost to the extreme to which their enemies' suspicions thought they were tending, and they claimed the immediate and supreme authority for what they believed and practiced, irrespective of any scriptural sanction.

What we can study in the clear light of history in the seventeenth century happened *mutatis mutandis* in the first century. Certainly the followers of Jesus found themselves left with an unresolved problem on their hands in the matter of the scope and extent of Old Testament authority in the new movement, and Jesus most likely combined, much as the early Quakers did, an independence of judgment with a sense of complete fidelity to the official scriptures and to their generally accepted authority. In both instances their critics could not reconcile the two aspects of the combination and made the most of every implicit belittling of the traditional standard.

We must come back to Jesus and to the proper subject of this chapter, the modernizing of his religious experience. Less than some others was this aspect of Jesus a matter of interest to the early Christians. The epistle to the Hebrews has some interest in the religious experience of Jesus. It speaks of his temptation, of his cries and prayers to God, of his sinlessness, of his learning by what he suffered. All this sounds very much like human religious experience and it has often been supposed to come from the actual traditions of the earthly Jesus. But whether historically accurate or not, history is not the ground of the writer's statements, but theory.

CHAP. VII  *The Religion of Jesus*

For him Jesus is a high priest taken from among men, and the requirements of such a high priest are for this author logical necessities based upon his view of "atonement through sympathy."

In the Fourth Gospel also a religious experience of Jesus is presented. It is an intimate fellowship, harmony and communion with the Father. There is perfect unity of knowledge, will and purpose between them. The passages to this effect are abundant and familiar. Their impressive character cannot guarantee them as historical self-disclosures. They are much more the attribution to Jesus of a mystical relation which the author himself has felt. He believed that Jesus stood towards God, as the Christian stands towards Jesus. The God-mysticism of the former is deduced from the Christ-mysticism of the latter. The process is not reversed.

In both these writings the experience of Jesus is significant not in itself nor even as a model for the believer. It is significant because of the place that Jesus holds in the believer's own religion. And this is even more exclusively the interest in the rest of the New Testament. Jesus is the object rather than subject of religious experience.

Paul, for example, considers the relation of Jesus to God quite from the outside. What God meant to Jesus, how it felt to be the Messiah, were questions of historical psychology that did not interest Paul. The same objectivity is almost equally true of the synoptic evangelists. Now that human curiosity has been roused and the question of Jesus' religious consciousness has been raised, men turn to these synoptic records to try to penetrate the mystery behind their objective exterior. For more than a generation this curiosity has been concerned primarily with one unique phase of that religious self-consciousness, namely, with Messiahship. That is indeed a fascinating problem and worthy of all the effort that has been spent upon it, even if with no certain results. But what of his general religious experience?

Here as much as anywhere in our study we are handicapped by the lack of evidence. How incomplete and imperfect a picture the gospel writers give of the religious personality of Jesus may be conjectured by the situation we are in when we consider Paul, from whom we have not only a clear narrative and vivid addresses from the pen of one of these same writers, but his own letters as well. "If we had such letters from Jesus," comments Professor Porter, "how many of our painful questions would be answered. When we read the stories about Paul in the Book of Acts, important and reliable in the main though they are, and then turn to Paul's letters, we realize how much of his personality vanishes when we have him at secondhand, even

CHAP. VII  *The Religion of Jesus*

though the hand may be that of an intimate friend and loyal disciple. The most original of Paul's thoughts, the highest ranges of his feeling and imagination, almost all that was greatest in him, we know from the letters alone. In them we have Paul himself." [7]

There are two or three groups of synoptic passages which seem to draw us very near to the religious experience of Jesus. They are the temptation passage, the voices from heaven, and the references to Jesus at prayer. These include the baptism, the transfiguration, and the scene in Gethsemane.

The first impression one gets of some of these is that they are distinctly psychic experiences. Indeed they have even been used as basis for elaborate theories of the abnormal character of Jesus. Modern mystics find in them the visions and voices characteristic of the mystic way, and have inferred from them that Jesus lived in the occasional guidance of direct divine communication. Outstanding are the baptism and transfiguration scenes. They contain not merely auditory but visual phenomena. The Holy Spirit descends as a dove. Moses transfigured and Elijah appear, not only to Jesus but to the three disciples.

We must grant the possibility that these stories portray, much as Jesus would have described it, what actually occurred. His description would be in accord with the religious presupposition of himself, his disci-

*The Peril of Modernizing Jesus*     CHAP. VII

ples and his contemporaries. So also would be the retelling of it by witnesses or later tradition. There seems to be some evidence of the association of a dove with the Spirit in Judaism and of an expectation of the return of Moses, Enoch and Elijah, or at least two of them, in preparation for the Messiah. In spite of the theoretical cessation of prophecy, the concept of direct divine communication is attested by rabbinic stories which claim circumstantially just such auditions. All that the New Testament lacks is the curious technical Wordsworthian-sounding phrase used by the rabbis, *bath qol,* or "daughter of a voice."

Yet one cannot feel too confident of the inner meaning of these concretely described episodes. Their value to the evangelists who relate them is not religious biography but religious evidence. As another evangelist says in similar circumstances, they are not for Jesus' own sake but for those who stand by and (we may add) for the readers of the account afterwards. Christian tradition naturally demanded some direct divine imprimatur on the career of Jesus and supplied it in the very terms which would suit the presuppositions of its own experience. Even these episodes are in a sense a primitive modernizing of Jesus, and since their meaning to the evangelists is apologetic and evidential, we are prevented from passing behind the form in

CHAP. VII  *The Religion of Jesus*

which they are told to a firsthand experience of Jesus himself.

We need hardly remind ourselves that the baptism of Jesus is not told without the Christian experience of baptism in mind. For him, as for his followers, it must be a rite with water, but with the Holy Spirit as well. The arrival of the Spirit is regarded as a definite experience. Luke's account compared with Acts shows the easy way in which Christianity tended to assimilate the episodes of Jesus' life with the practices or experiences of the church.

In another way the baptism of Jesus is much more than the report of an experience. The Messiah means "the anointed," and if Jesus is the Messiah, some evidence is required that he was literally anointed. The Messiah also must have his forerunner. In John the Baptist, and in his baptism of Jesus, Christianity found the fulfilment of these requirements. This interest rather than any appreciation of the inward significance determined the tradition preserved in our synoptic gospels of Jesus' baptism. How shall we then presume to analyze the inner life of Jesus from evidence whose selection and presentation had such a method and such a purpose?

We may feel disappointed if we cannot have confidence in the usual list of inner crises in the life of Jesus as they are inferred from the synoptic gospels in the books we read. If events like his baptism or the confession of Peter are not inward turning points in his career, certainly no other more trustworthy data for that inner life are forthcoming. Fear of the alternative of not knowing, however, is never a good argument for accepting ill-supported guesses.

Of Jesus' use of prayer there is no reason to entertain scepticism. That he engaged in prayer we could take for granted without the evidence of the gospels. In fact, that evidence again represents sometimes a Christian interest, or a Christian assumption, as when Luke associates it with the ceremony of baptism or with the choice of the twelve. Jesus' words about prayer may be some indication of his own experience in praying; but they assume prayer as practiced by the Jews about him. We must remember that the mere fact of prayer, while it marks Jesus as a religious person, hardly proves that religion was central in his life. Of the genuine religiousness of Jesus we have no doubt; the difficulty comes when we make out Jesus' practice of prayer according to our own ideal of prayer. He recommends trust, persistence, brevity, humility, repentance, forgiveness, and privacy as proper traits in prayer. We can see that his own practice is not always construed by modern Christians in these terms. He discouraged repetition, but at Gethsemane uttered the same prayer

CHAP. VII  *The Religion of Jesus*

thrice, he criticized long prayers of Pharisees but continued, himself, all night in prayer. The data about prayer have in each place their own motives in the tradition.

Some of us find it hard to suppose that Jesus practiced fasting and almsgiving as part of his Jewish piety. The gospel evidence is less abundant but that is not really significant. The Sermon on the Mount associates all three in good Jewish fashion and gives similar advice about their practice. It is the disciples of Jesus who are said not to fast and not Jesus, and the reference to them seems like later controversy. The common contrast with John the Baptist that makes Jesus out so sociable and non-ascetic is almost certainly overdrawn. Jesus in a sense was probably ascetic, yet neither in a medieval nor in a modern sense but in a way characteristic of Judaism. The aim of his asceticism was not self-discipline but obedience to God, and both almsgiving and fasting were very much like prayer as being offered to God as appeals for his regard and favor.

In the absence of definite data we can say nothing about Jesus' sense of sin. That he was without sin is a later theological assumption. The first evangelists had no reason with their interests either to affirm or to deny sinlessness of him. Apart from John's gospel, the only relevant saying is the demurrer: "Why callest thou me good? None is good save one, even God." The spiritual depression due to sin was not unknown in the ancient world, but human nature was such that the fear of the consequent divine punishment usually overshadowed it. The morbid gnawing of an uneasy conscience seems improbable from the little we can infer of the temperament of Jesus or from the emotional patterns of contemporary Judaism.

Particularly poignant in our time is the sense of corporate sin. We feel this sin not so much in our individual acts as in sharing, or condoning; in committing almost unavoidably the wholesale crimes by which society organizes "man's inhumanity to man." We almost envy Jesus or any other idealist to whom sin is only that which the individual commits. In spite of the ancient prophets' ability to picture sin in the wholesale, the sin of the nation we can hardly assign to Jesus as something that he shared. Even Paul and the author of Second Esdras, who are nearly contemporary with Jesus and reflect contemporary Jewish ideas, when they think of the pitiful plight of sinful mankind hastening to the doom of its wholesale guilt, do not include themselves. Their responsibility is from the outside, like watchmen, to warn individuals to repent. This absence in Jesus of corporate guilt corresponds to the second limitation of his social outlook mentioned in an earlier chapter. In contrast with us, one says of him: "New forms of sin, particularly the baffling forms of corpo-

CHAP. VII *The Religion of Jesus*

rate sin, which mark the modern age, would have been left wholly out of view."[8]

Passing now to the less tangible phases of religious experience, we may safely infer that the religion of Jesus emphasized the passive element in a way that we should find only partially congenial. Religion for Jesus is much more what God does than what man does. Certainly God makes the decisions of most importance. What we should think rather passive or fatalistic may well have been the attitude of Jesus. The important thing for man is to accept the divine ordering. "Not my will but thine be done" is the prayer that fits not only Gethsemane but every day. In the teaching of Jesus to others there is a similar unmistakable trend. Resignation, forbearance, acceptance and endurance are not so much virtues selected among a wider list: they are typical of the beatitudes as a whole and of Jesus' whole teaching in denying self, self-interest, self-defence, self-assertion. Jesus' relation with God was not active and eager coöperation but loyal acceptance of what God determined.

Akin to this is a quite different idea of divine guidance. It is not a search for God's recommendations, it is the recognition of his decisions. Guidance is not asking God, what shall I do next? It is rather asking God whether this or that may not be his will. So prayer is not a prayer for light but a prayer for strength and obedience. We do not learn God's will by fresh direct revelations for our initiative, but his will for us personally he reveals to us step by step in what he lets happen to us. Of course in a general way his will is alike for all men. That is the standard of the Jewish law. It is sufficient guidance for us in so far as we have any active duties to fulfill. Faithfulness in this will is something that Jesus seems to have taken for granted for himself. No doubt he practiced such faithfulness as he understood the law to mean; no doubt he had come to feel the manner of life and character that it implied. Obedience, however, to such a standard requires no frequent personal revelations from God. We ourselves communicate to God in prayer our needs and counter-requirements.

If Jesus believed himself Messiah, the idea came to him in accordance with this religious practice. Messiahship was not something he took upon himself; God put it upon him, and God's selection of him for that office would be known to him in the same passive way just described. God's will is known by interpreting what happens. In so far as you can foresee what will happen, you can anticipate that will; in so far as you can understand what has happened, you can acknowledge that will.

The species of resignation is typically oriental, we westerners would say. It was characteristically Jewish.

CHAP. VII  *The Religion of Jesus*

Although we are familiar with its expression in Jeremiah and the Psalms, we frequently overlook it in Jesus. Possibly his outlook on his death shows it most clearly: "I cast out demons and perform cures today and tomorrow and the third day I am perfected. Nevertheless, I must go on my way today and tomorrow and the day following; for it cannot be that a prophet perish out of Jerusalem." It would be wrong to suppose that it is only towards evil that one takes the passive view. A Jew would be passive to good too. We call it dependence or faith but they are much the same. "Be it unto me according to thy word" is acceptance of good as of evil, and Jesus moved through the vicissitudes of life with this rather unmodern type of religion.

There are many important ramifications of this seemingly negative and passive religious self-consciousness. It explains many features in Jesus' life and sayings which we deal with usually quite artificially to make them fit our standards. It means that much of our reconstruction contains psychological anachronisms or inaccuracies. No doubt much Christian apologetic colors the evangelists' quotations of the scriptures, but perhaps Jesus himself felt that a kind of ordained destiny controlled their fulfilment. Even apart from scripture, how men respond to his message, how they fail to understand the parables, why many are called and few chosen, are quite as much religious necessities as his own career. With the usual human dualistic assumptions of free will and predestination, the religion of Jesus assumes both, but because of its underlying basic theism and of its interpretation of the divine will in its personal aspect as an overruling providence, the fatalistic acceptance of what God disposes plays an important part.

In this as in other respects the religion of Jesus is not introspective and subjective but rather objective. The part of religion one looks at within is one's own degree of fidelity in keeping the well-known standards of the divine will. The rest of religion is external. Probably Jesus neither taught nor felt the importance of a religious experience. He did not live in the ecstatic moment, nor glory in it, nor even in the more normal sense of abiding fellowship with God. Whatever we make out of the famous saying about the mutual knowledge of Son and Father, it can hardly be correlated with our modern emphasis on experience.

The opinions here stated cannot be definitely proved any more than can their opposites. We are so likely to think that just as again and again later, when Christianity has become dead and formal, fresh life has come through leaders who bring men to new religious experience, Jesus himself did the same for men in first-century Judaism. Undoubtedly Jews and Gentiles also in those days did, as Christians, attain a much deeper

## The Religion of Jesus

religious experience than they had before, but probably not because Jesus' precept or his example led them to do so. It was rather the religion about Jesus. Jesus himself made religious experience no aim or goal in his own life or in his teaching. Never consciously at least would he have emphasized experience as something valuable and to be enriched. Nor should we attribute his own achievement to some peculiarly vigorous struggle for communication with God or peculiarly clear consciousness of God. He understood God's will differently from many Jews. His moral intuitions were keen and sensitive, no doubt. But that quality does not depend on what we so glibly call, without definition, "religious experience."

Many scholars who will admit that Jesus was not a mystic in the sense that the word commonly conveys of ecstasies, auditions, trances, and other psychic phenomena, nevertheless claim for him a more rational sort of mysticism. In particular they assert that God was much more real to him than to others, that he felt a particular fellowship with his Father, and that no one ever understood quite so perfectly the divine will.[9]

To a very large extent such a superlative description needs no refutation. It is pure rhetoric without any real foundation. It merely indicates what the modern writer wishes to read between the lines of the gospel story because it is his own ideal. Certainly one cannot derive it from the references to God in Jesus' own teaching. They are not very frequent in the synoptic gospels. The fixed phrase, "Kingdom of God," accounts for more than half of them. Even when God is mentioned Jesus does not make him central in his teaching. That teaching is about human conduct. When Jesus mentions God's care for the lilies and birds he is not aiming primarily at a new definition of God. He appeals to a familiar and obvious fact in nature and what he is really concerned about is the foolishness of men's worrying.

God then is not in the foreground of Jesus' thinking, but in the background. Such a place for God may be religious, even more religious than is conscious thought about him or frequent prating with his name. Jesus lived in a community that took God quite for granted. For such persons to name the name of God has nothing of the same distinctive mark of religiousness that it might have elsewhere. Anyone familiar with the Moslem world must be aware that it is possible to have God's name on one's lips constantly without any corresponding special piety as we should expect it. The easier and more natural the reality of God to such people the less it carries with it many of the most prized elements of modern religion—spiritual awareness, conscious piety, appreciated fellowship, faith and love.

As Professor Macdonald says of the earlier Hebrews,

## The Religion of Jesus

"God was tremendously real and distinct—next in reality to their own selves. . . . They often were not at all what we would call pious, or regenerate or religious minded, but as to God they had no shadow of doubt. This explains the extreme simplicity with which, throughout, they accept him and treat him. . . . For the old Hebrews our secular and sacred were also one. The supernatural and the natural were also one; the only difference then was of the invisible and the visible; and these two were equally real." [10]

That Jesus knew God more intimately than other men is not supported by the gospel evidence. We infer it because what Jesus became in later theology requires it and particularly because we think of his judgments as being independent and correct and therefore we assume communicated to him by God. It is doubtful whether even when Jesus was most aware of differing from his contemporaries he would have made any such claim for himself. His confident views of right and wrong were not due in his own eyes to special knowledge that God had vouchsafed, neither did he urge his followers to look to God to reveal his will in them. He did not proclaim a revival of direct revelation as in the prophets, though his followers often claimed it for themselves as well as for him. It was not new knowledge that men needed. Jesus took for granted that they knew what was right already. He regarded the law as containing all that was necessary by way of divine communication. Men often failed to practice its most significant requirements, more out of wilfulness than any failure to understand, but it never occurred to him that their natural faculties needed any supernatural supplementing. He did not need it himself, why expect it for others? His own understanding of the divine will in the law and the prophets seemed to him inevitable. It was inevitable then for him to proclaim it. Do we really need to add in order to understand him considerations which were not conscious to him? Even if we do, we must recall that it is our interpretation rather than his own.

In brief what is said in this chapter both first and last may be summed up in a single sentence. The religion of Jesus was not centered about a specifically religious experience. It was rather the religious interpretation of unspecifically religious experience—his homely knowledge of men and of nature, his native and forthright sense of good and evil, and his personal acceptance of the life that befell him with its twofold prospects of success and failure as the divine will for him.

The demodernizing of Jesus at first sight seems a destructive and disappointing process. It leaves us an historical figure and an historical scene vague and in-

CHAP. VII  *The Religion of Jesus*

complete in outline, jejune in interest, alien and irrelevant to the great issues of modern life. How shall we fill the gap that is left? To import merely a different and a more modern view, to read into the unfilled portrait the new tastes, to wax eloquent with new superlatives, will not improve the situation. This would too much resemble Jesus' own parable of the man from whom the unclean spirit is exorcised only to be re-entered by that spirit and by seven worse ones. The gap must either be left empty or be filled partially and tentatively by painstaking historical research and imagination. That is the task of all history; the evangelic episode is no unique one. First the labor of criticism and research, and then the artistic, poetic reconstruction. As Wilamowitz has finely said, comparing the modern with the ancient historian:

We ourselves, when once Dryasdust [*i.e.*, research] has done his work within us, and we advance to the shaping of our scientific results—from that time forth we do just the same, we use our free formative imagination. The tradition yields us only ruins. The more closely we test and examine them, the more clearly we see how ruinous they are; and of ruins no whole can be built. The tradition is dead; our task is to revivify that life that has passed away. We know that ghosts cannot speak until they have drunk blood, and the spirits which we evoke demand the blood of our hearts. We give it to them gladly; but if they there abide our question, something from us has entered into them; something alien, that must be cast out, cast out in the name of truth! [11]

In addition to the temptation to modernize, the figure of Jesus offers another way of filling the gap in our historical knowledge, a way that is as old as the gospels themselves. In spite of all their objectivity the Jesus of the gospels is not and was not meant to be merely a figure of history. He is for them and for every early Christian an object of religious faith. The relation of religion and history, of faith and fact, presents a problem that cannot be disposed of in a few words, but it is evident to any one who knows his New Testament that this volume represents an inseparable synthesis of faith and history. Modern Christians follow suit unconsciously and even with quite self-conscious insistence. They insist that even as historical students we must not omit the Christ of faith. Apart from his continued work in the church (Gemeinde), writes Wellhausen, "we can form no conception of the religious personality of Jesus." [12] A more recent German writer declares in words that many would endorse:

The Jesus of history is valueless and unintelligible unless he be experienced and confessed by faith as the living Christ. . . . These two are utterly inseparable in the New Testament. They cannot even be thought of apart. . . .

CHAP. VII  *The Religion of Jesus*

Anyone who attempts first to separate the two and then to describe only one of them has nothing in common with the New Testament.[13]

Is it possible to read out of court the effort to regain the historical Jesus, just because it is not the effort of the New Testament? Certainly Jesus of Nazareth needs no special pleading or exemption from the canons of historical study. For many of us it will remain more satisfactory to leave much about him unknown, much about him alien both to ourselves and to the church that more immediately succeeded him, than to paint him up unconcernedly in our own image, or what becomes so often quite similar, to attempt to supplement the imperfect historical portrait with what we call the Christ of faith. Religious faith has its place, but it is doing no service to either religion or science to allow religious faith the authority which belongs to history, or vice versa. Both faith and history have their gaps, but they do not exactly supplement each other. Rather history illustrates faith and faith interprets history. Without illegitimate borrowings between them we may follow both as far as each will lead us.

# NOTES

## CHAPTER I

1. I had in mind here the Ryks Museum at Amsterdam, but I have played this little game in several places, with different schools or periods of art.
2. H. B. Workman, *Persecution in the Early Church*, Sharp, 1906, p. 73.
3. Brown-Serman and Prichard, *What did Jesus Think?* Macmillan, 1935, p. 35.
4. Bruce Barton, *The Man Nobody Knows*, Bobbs Merrill, 1925, pp. 195 ff. In all fairness it must be said that the book was written with reverence and from a sincere desire to deal appreciatively with Jesus. This is, however, no guarantee of historical appropriateness.
5. Brown-Serman and Prichard, *op. cit.*, p. 142.
6. Bruce Barton, *op. cit.*, pp. 104, 126, 127.
7. *Ibid.*, p. 162. The italics are not from the Authorized Version, though it might well have italicized "business" to indicate, after its usual manner, that there is no such word here in the original Greek, only an article!
8. Charles Gore, *Jesus of Nazareth*, Holt; T. Butterworth, 1929, p. 67.
9. T. N. Carver, "The Economic Factor in the Messiahship of Jesus," in *The Christian Register*, ci. (1922), pp. 101 ff.
10. A. Schweitzer, *The Quest of the Historical Jesus*, Eng. Trans., Macmillan; Black, 1910, p. 397.
11. Such a formula, most familiar from Acts 20:35, is more

*Notes* CHAP. I

abundant in the first two Christian centuries than is commonly realized. See the list of passages conveniently collected in H. G. Evelyn White, *The Sayings of Jesus from Oxyrhynchus,* Macmillan, 1920, p. xxx f., or the note on Acts 20:35 in *The Beginnings of Christianity,* by Lake and Jackson, Macmillan, Vol. IV., 1933.

12. Matt. 3:15; Hebrews 2:17.

13. See the classic discussion by D. W. Riddle of "The Martyr Motive in the Gospel according to Mark," *The Journal of Religion,* iv, 1924, pp. 397 ff., and the same writer's fuller treatment in his book, *The Martyrs, a Study in Social Control,* Univ. of Chicago Press; Cambridge Univ. Press, 1931.

14. Luke 23:34a omitted by weighty early authorities; Acts 7:60.

15. Mark 2:18 f., 23 f.; 7:1 f.

16. I am glad to call attention to a volume published since these pages were written, Martin Dibelius, *Gospel Criticism and Christology,* Nicholson, 1935, in which much is well said including many points in these last paragraphs.

## CHAPTER II

1. The frequent claims of eternal contemporaneity for Jesus may be illustrated by a single quotation:

One of the world's greatest stories is that of *The Wandering Jew*. It is a story which symbolizes a profound truth of Christian history. The hero of this medieval tale is one who is supposed to be condemned by Jesus to immortality on earth. He can never retire completely from the human scene, but must reappear in each new generation as its contemporary. In a high and reverent sense Jesus is the Wandering Jew. He does not come upon the scene in each new century as a Rip Van Winkle, but as the contemporary of each new age, the one in whom its highest aspirations find fulfillment. When the age

CHAP. II *Notes*

of democracy came on the world's calendar, it found in Jesus its highest exponent and leader. So it is with many other characteristics of our time. (H. E. Luccock, *Jesus and the American Mind,* Abingdon Press, 1930, pp. 49 f.).

2. The legitimate citation of Jesus for our own ideas is well described in contrast with the illegitimate in a review written by S. J. Case, "Rival Efforts to Modernize Jesus," dealing with a Ritschlian and a Barthian example (*The Journal of Religion,* xv, 1935, pp. 82 ff.). I quote from the beginning and the end:

"The attempt to capture the historical Jesus for one or another type of later Christian opinion is a time-honored quest. The chase still goes merrily on. . . . One who reads these two books side by side will easily perceive that both authors attempt to give vital reality to Jesus by depicting him in the religious imagery that accords most nearly with their respective tastes. It is the privilege, indeed the duty of the religious man of today to express his opinions and ideals in terms of the deepest realities of his own experience within his specific environment. . . . He is also entitled to draw support for his views from as wide a range of historical data as may be available to him, whether he resorts to Jesus, Paul, the evangelists, or any other notable persons of the past. As a selective and interpretative procedure, if so understood, his performance need not cause offense to anyone. But if he assumes that his presentation represents the totality of any given historical phenomenon, like the life and teaching of Jesus, or that his interpretation is the only justifiable one, then his readers have the right to demur."

3. See my article, "The Social Translation of the Gospel," in the *Harvard Theological Review,* xv, 1922, 1 ff. The more objective method is not likely to be popular and the easy-going present day modernization of Jesus will continue until it is discarded for a more modern modernization of a succeeding generation.

## *Notes* CHAP. II

4. One does not have to share the Roman standpoint of Father Tyrrell to sympathize with his criticism of *What is Christianity?* He says: "The Christ that Harnack sees, looking back through nineteen centuries of Catholic darkness, is only the reflection of a Liberal Protestant face, seen at the bottom of a deep well." (*Christianity at the Cross Roads*, Longmans, London, 1909, p. 44.)

5. Matt. 27:27-31.

6. Of course a great deal depends on *how* the gospels are used or studied. Practical considerations have only too often led to ignoring the ancient Jewish character of the material, and the whole science may be regarded as a series of successive modernizations, since it is supposed that the results must have validity for the student's own day. Even some of the most modern and critical German studies are plainly tinged with Barthianism just as the earlier American books were a naive reading back to Jesus of our "social gospel." There is some reason to hope that certain of the styles of gospel criticism, *Formgeschichte* (form criticism) and the social or environmental interpretation of the evangelic material, by recalling us to the early influences contemporary with Jesus or the evangelists, will obviate some temptations towards modernization. See the article by D. W. Riddle on "The Bearing of Recent Gospel Research upon the Study of the Teaching of Jesus" in *The Journal of Religion*, xiv (1934), pp. 150 f.

While speaking of method I cannot refrain from quoting some of the excellent words of C. H. Dodd in his recent inaugural lecture in which he meets the easy going assumption that one can find the permanent in Jesus by ignoring the temporary or contemporary. He says:

Our study is in the first place historical, for it aims at the interpretation of that significant phenomenon in history which is early Christianity. Such study is peculiarly relevant to a religion which so emphatically announces itself as an historical revelation. But the interpreter I have in mind will be one who, having penetrated to the historical actuality of the first-century Christianity, has received an impression of the truth in it which lies beyond the flux of time, and demands to be restated in terms intelligible to the mind of our own age. It is not that the thought of the twentieth century is, as such, superior in validity to that of the first century, but that no truth can be communicated, or even fully grasped, until it can be naturalized, in any age whatever.

The problem of interpretation has not been fully comprehended, to my mind, if it be conceived as an attempt to disengage (according to a popular formula) the "permanent" element in the New Testament from its "temporary" setting. . . . No attempt to extract particular elements from it, and to exhibit these as "permanent" in isolation from the rest, can be other than superficial. . . .

The ideal interpreter would be one who has entered into that strange first-century world, has felt its whole strangeness, has sojourned in it until he has lived himself into it, thinking and feeling as one of those to whom the Gospel first came; and who will then return into our world, and give to the truth he has discerned a body out of the stuff of our own thought. (*The Present Task in New Testament Studies*, Macmillan; Cambridge Univ. Press, 1936, 37 ff.)

## CHAPTER III

1. *Journal of Theological Studies*, xxxiii (1931), p. 66.

2. In glancing recently at a local college weekly I noted a writer's rather fresh phrase: "But in this little article I do not propose to empty the ocean with a spoon." Its unfamiliarity was at once explained when I looked back to see who wrote the article—a visiting professor from Italy.

3. For these parallels compare my *Making of Luke-Acts*, p. 148 n. To his article there mentioned G. B. King has added "A Further Note on the Mote and the Beam," *Harvard Theological Review*, xxvi (1933), pp. 73 ff.

## Notes  CHAP. III

4. Of course it is not only the form of the parables which shows contemporary color. Their contents give a very full picture of contemporary life in Palestine, superior to anything obtainable from any other ancient popular source except the papyri of Egypt. See C. H. Dodd, *The Authority of the Bible,* Harper; Nisbet, 1928, pp. 147-152. A very apologetic use of this material is made in A. M. Fairbairn, *The Philosophy of the Christian Religion,* Macmillan, 1902, pp. 383-386. See the whole passage beginning, "His discourses have so marvellous a hold on reality that their place, their time, and their whole social environment may be seen reflected as in a mirror," and ending, "The whole Jewish world is there, a compact, coherent, living world, which we can re-articulate, re-vivify, and visualize, even though the magic mirror in which we behold it is the teaching which reveals the kingdom of Heaven."

5. On the *a fortiori* argument among the Jews called *ḳal wechomer,* see *Encyclopaedia Judaica,* vii. 1931, col. 1185 ff.

6. Sanhedrin 90*b* as translated in Billerbeck, *Kommentar zum N. T.* i. 895. For this and the following examples compare A. Marmorstein, "The Doctrine of the Resurrection of the Dead in Rabbinical Theology," *American Journal of Theology,* xix (1915), pp. 577-591.

7. Genesis Rabba 14 (10*c*) referring of course to Gen. 2:7, and other passages in Billerbeck, *loc.cit.*

8. Matt. 21:31; Matt. 21:40; Luke 7:42; Luke 10:36.

9. The incident is related again in the passage previously quoted (Sanhedrin 90*b*) and elsewhere. The questioner is called Queen Cleopatra. See Billerbeck, *op.cit.,* i.897; G. F. Moore, *Judaism in the First Centuries of the Christian Era,* Harvard Univ. Press, ii.381.

10. Exod. 3:6. Characteristically different use of the same text in Exodus is made by the writer to the Hebrews (11:16). He does not actually quote Exodus, but he must have it in mind when he writes of the patriarchs that their faith makes

CHAP. III  *Notes*

plain that they seek a homeland, and that a heavenly one. "Wherefore God is not ashamed to be called their God: for he hath prepared for them a city." In calling himself the God of Abraham, Isaac and Jacob, God is accepting and satisfying their desire for immortality. The city that is their future homeland he has already prepared. If it were not so (cf. John 14:2) it would be a reflection either on him or on them and he would be ashamed to be called their God.

11. G. F. Moore, *Judaism in the First Centuries of the Christian Era*, ii.382, using Sanhedrin 90*b*. The verse is Deut. 11:9. Moore explains in a note, "The patriarchs were dead before the occupation of the land; God's oath could only be fulfilled by raising them from the dead."

12. G. F. Moore points out the interesting fact that the texts in our hands today of both the Samaritan Pentateuch and its Targum omit the words "to them" in Deut. 11:9.

13. Num. 18:28.

## CHAPTER IV

1. Mark 1:21-28. Joshua Starr in his note on "The Meaning of 'Authority' in Mark 1:22" in the *Harvard Theological Review*, xxiii, 1930, 302 ff., is certainly on the right track in giving the word a thaumaturgic sense. Cf. Mark 2:10; 3:15; 6:7; 11:28 ff.

2. Albert Schweitzer, *Paul and His Interpreters, a Critical History*. Eng. Trans., Macmillan; Black, 1912, p. x.

The recognition of the archaic and Jewish in Jesus does not in itself belittle him except for those who regard greatness as synonymous either with the modern or with the universal. Such a view is, however, common.

The protests of two German modernists may be quoted. H. Weinel, *Ist das 'liberale' Jesusbild widerlegt?* 1910, p. 36, affirms after Wellhausen, "Man darf das Nichtjüdische an ihm, das Menschliche für charakteristischer halten als das Jüdische."

*Notes* CHAP. IV

A. Harnack (*What is Christianity?* Eng. Trans., Williams & Norgate; American Edition, Putnam, 1901, p. 58) complains: "It is considered a perverse procedure in similar cases to judge eminent, epoch-making personalities first and foremost by what they share with their contemporaries, and on the other hand to put what is great and characteristic in them into the background. The tendency as far as possible to reduce everything to one level and to efface what is special and individual may spring in some minds from a praiseworthy sense of truth, but it has proved misleading. More frequently, however, we get the endeavour to refuse greatness any recognition at all, and to throw down anything that is exalted." Obviously the demodernizing of Jesus can be so abused. But the danger of this abuse is no excuse for minimizing his historical unmodernness.

3. Mark 1:37 f. Other passages appealed to in this connection are Luke 10:20 and 11:24 ff. (with its parallel).

4. According to Luke 4:18, contrast Mark 6:2.

5. On contemporary miracles see Paul Fiebig, *Jüdische Wundergeschichten des neutestamentlichen Zeitalters,* u.s.w., 1911. On exorcism see among others Campbell Bonner, "Traces of Thaumaturgic Technique in the Miracles," *Harvard Theological Review,* xx, 1927, pp. 171 ff. For Aramaic in cures: Mark 5:41; 7:34; in prayers: Mark 14:36; 15:34.

## CHAPTER V

1. The quotations come from Shailer Mathews, *The Social Teaching of Jesus,* Macmillan, 1897, pages 54, 58, 58, 59, 62, 34-36. In quoting from this book I gladly recognize that the author has not always pressed the social gospel so far. He himself has recanted or at least replaced his earlier work with his *Jesus on Social Institutions,* Macmillan, 1928. See also his books, *The Social Gospel,* Amer. Bapt., 1910, and *The Individual and*

*the Social Gospel,* 1914. Typical too of the late Professor Peabody was his conviction in spite of the immense sale of his *Jesus Christ and the Social Question,* Macmillan (1900), that a much better and truer book was his *Jesus Christ and the Christian Character* (1905). For a history of the literature see Shailer Mathews, "The Development of Social Christianity in America during the Past Twenty-Five Years," in the *Journal of Religion,* vii, 1927, 376 ff. A generation ago a favorite *bon mot* among American scholars was to·the effect that socialist Germany had substituted for the Gospel of Mark the gospel of Marx; perhaps one could reply that modernist America has substituted for the Gospel of Matthew the Gospel of Mathews!

After forty years the fallacy still continues. We read into Jesus *our* modern social gospel and then we note with triumph that *his* gospel of the Kingdom has at last been recovered:

"Jesus and his gospel have suddenly come back in our day. The Master stands before us again in all his power and beauty; his gospel has emerged from its long eclipse. For Jesus is more near and real to our generation than he has been since he lived in Galilee. . . . With a strange sense of nearness we find him walking by our side the highways of life as he did long ago in Palestine. The Great Galilean has returned." (H. K. Booth, *The Great Galilean Returns,* Scribner, 1936, p. viii.)

2. "There has never been any inconvenient crowd at the narrow gate. In every generation many are called, but few chosen." Dean W. R. Inge, *The Gate of Life,* Longmans, 1935.

3. "It is inconceivable that Jesus could have taught a gospel of sonship with the Father—sonship in which, as we have seen, all men potentially share—and yet have taught individualism." (Brown-Serman and Prichard, *What Did Jesus Think?* Macmillan, 1935, p. 182.)

4. If this still needs proof see Moore, *Judaism in the First*

*Notes* CHAP. V

*Centuries of the Christian Era,* ii.201-211; Billerbeck, *op.cit.* i.392-6. Strange how many liberal scholars try to have it both ways at once with Jesus' use of the word "Father," claiming from it proof both that Jesus really felt that God's relation was of a loving parent to all men alike, and that he was father to Jesus uniquely, as to no one else.

5. "Jesus lived in an age when despotism was regnant; and yet he was the most thorough-going democrat that has appeared in human history." (C. F. Kent, *The Social Teachings of the Prophets and Jesus,* Scribner, 1917, p. 254.)

In the index to *A Social Theory of Religious Education,* by George A. Coe, published in 1917 (Scribner)—note the date as in the preceding—I find this cross reference, "Kingdom of God, see *Democracy.*" I have not undertaken to collect the more recent statements about dictatorship and the Kingdom of God. But evidently the socio-theological styles are changing in this direction in some quarters in America as well as in Europe.

6. The four passages on divorce and remarriage are Matt. 5:32; 19:9; Mark 10:11 f.; Luke 16:18. The nearest to similar kinds of proscription would be Matt. 5:33 ff., 38 ff.

7. Ellwood, *The Reconstruction of Religion,* Macmillan, 1922, pp. 78, 84, 129, 183.

8. Luke 12:48; 7:47; 16:10; Matt. 6:15.

9. *Essays on the Social Gospel,* by Wilhelm Herrmann and Adolf Harnack, Eng. Trans., 1907, p. 12. The agraphon is from Origen, *in Matt.,* tom.xv.14, the next from Jerome, *in Ephes.*v.3 ff.

10. The joy after human service to which the canonical gospels refer is otherwise motivated: "In this rejoice not that the spirits are subject unto you; but rejoice that your names are written in heaven" (Luke 10:20).

11. Matt. 7:1; Mark 11:25; Luke 6:38; Matt. 6:14; Matt. 6:12; Luke 11:4; Matt. 5:7; Luke 6:36.

CHAP. V *Notes*

12. V. H. Stanton, *The Gospels as Historical Documents,* Macmillan, ii, 1909, p. 234 f.

13. Luke 12:58; Luke 16:9; Matt. 26:52; Luke 14:10.

14. E. F. Scott, *The Ethical Teaching of Jesus,* Macmillan, 1924, p. 60 f.

15. Matt. 6:4. Modern scruples are not relieved by the addition in late MSS of the word "openly," unless it be thought more appropriate for God to advertise his justice in rewarding almsgivers, than for them to advertise their gifts. As J. E. Carpenter, *First Three Gospels,* 1890, p. 68 f., explains: "Should not the world know that love and piety received their reward? In the interests of religion it was desirable that the blessing should be visible to all, and accordingly an amended version of the promise ran, 'Thy Father, who sees in secret, shall recompense thee *openly.*'" This is quoted by C. G. Montefiore, *The Synoptic Gospels,* second edition, Macmillan, 1927, ii.97, where he has some excellent things to say about the compatibility of belief in reward with disinterestedness and with being or doing good for the sake of goodness. For the rabbinic teaching of secret almsgiving (which Montefiore does not mention here, but in *Rabbinic Literature and Gospel Teachings,* Macmillan, 1930, pp. 111 ff.), see G. F. Moore, *Judaism,* ii. 167, 178 f. and the note in iii.188: "On almsgiving in secret see Baba Batra 9b. R. Eliezer deduces from two texts that the man who gives alms in secret is greater than Moses."

16. C. G. Montefiore, *The Old Testament and After,* Macmillan, 1923, p. 248. More than once elsewhere Montefiore is intrigued by the problem as presented by this passage: "We are not to resist the evil-doer. The reason is not wholly clear. Is it for the sake of a principle, or for our own sakes, or for the sake of the evil doer himself?" (*Hibbert Journal,* xx, 1922, p. 444.) "Jesus is thinking more of the recipient of an injury than of the man who does the wrong . . . the sufferer's right attitude." (*Rabbinic Literature and Gospel Teachings,* Mac-

millan, 1930, p. 51 f.) Cf. B. S. Easton, *Christ in the Gospels,* Scribner, 1930, p. 128, referring to Matt. 5:39 and Romans 12:20: "St. Paul gives us a motive based on benefiting the enemy, but Jesus does nothing of the sort: he gives us no motive beyond that of the saying itself, which concerns itself with nothing except the individual addressed. Since love is *my* paramount duty, *I* must practice love even under the most trying circumstances. *I* must turn the other cheek, surrender my coat, or bear the burden the second mile; as far as *I* am concerned, any resentment that would make *me* do otherwise is a sin. My primary concern is with my own motives and acts, and so my primal duty is to rid those motives and acts of selfishness." Of the parable of the Laborers in the Vineyard W. W. Fenn wrote (see Chap. VII, note 3): "Surely there are infelicities in the parable and not even Ruskin can fully satisfy us as to the economic truth of it. Yet Jesus was not speaking as an economist, nor—and here is the point of the parable—was he considering the matter from the point of view of the employer, but solely from the point of view of the man out of work."

17. The sensible words of two American teachers may be quoted:

On detailed solutions of modern social problems Jesus is silent for clear historical reasons. Standards in the social scale, wage adjustments, sharing the profits of production, ownership of natural resources, rights and responsibilities of capital and labor, etc., are problems that did not exist for him.

We cannot modernize Jesus and force him to speak our language and think our thoughts after us. We must have him in his own historical setting . . . to think his own thoughts and express them in the idioms of his own language in his own way. . . . We must learn to understand Jesus in the light of his own historical background. Thereby we shall find that much that is foreign, or even repulsive, to us today in the thought and teaching of Jesus belongs to the local color of

CHAP. V *Notes*

Jesus' historical background and day. (W. E. Bundy, *The Psychic Health of Jesus*, Macmillan, 1922, p. 146.)

In consideration of the social implications of Jesus' teaching the necessity for the utmost care and honesty in dealing with the records must be stressed. A constantly recurring feature of Christian history has been a forcible capture of Jesus. The scene in the Garden of Gethsemane, when he is overpowered by the Roman soldiers and forced to go along with them has been repeated again and again. He has been captured by the forces of the ecclesiasticism and his words warped into the support of positions which he assailed all his life. In a like manner he has been captured for absolutist theories of political power, for militarism, and materialistic economics. Also he has been forcibly impressed into the support of particular theories of social reform. In the cause of thoroughgoing ethical and social reconstruction of society men have dragged Jesus along with them. They have read back into his teaching ideas quite foreign to his time and to his own thought forms. Such excessive zeal is as mistaken as any other form of dishonesty. (H. E. Luccock, *Jesus and the American Mind*, Abingdon Press, 1930, p. 39 f.)

18. J. Moffatt, *The Approach to the N.T.*, Hodder & Stoughton, 1921, p. 173.

19. *Atlantic Monthly*, April, 1923, pp. 461 f. The example of modernizing Jesus along social lines most widely read at the present moment (1937) in both Great Britain and America is probably the chapter on "The Religion of Jesus" in John Macmurray's *Creative Society*. It has been admirably exposed and answered by his fellow-countryman, Alan Richardson, in a brief article entitled, "Was Jesus a Social Reformer?" in *Radical Religion*, ii, 1936, pp. 18-24.

## CHAPTER VI

1. Not every biographer of Jesus so obviously accepts the presupposition of purpose as does Bernhard Weiss. Rejecting

*Notes*

the older idea of a period utterly wanting in historical sense that Jesus devised a plan for the improvement of religion, morals and society by convincing instructions and by institutions, he nevertheless declared: "In common life it is considered a sign of immaturity for one to commence a public activity without being clear about his object and the means for its attainment. We must therefore suppose that Jesus did not appear without distinct knowledge of his calling," etc. *The Life of Christ*, Eng. Trans., Scribner, 1883, i., p. 295. Compare C. Guignebert, *Jesus*, Eng. Trans., Knopf; Routledge; Musson, 1935, p. 296: "It is legitimate to suppose, *a priori*, that the preaching of Jesus was characterized by a main purpose."

2. *The Aim of Jesus Christ*, by W. F. Cooley, Macmillan, 1925. Compare the title, *The Purpose of Jesus in the First Three Gospels*, by C. N. Moody, Harper; G. Allen, 1930.

3. Max Weber, *The Protestant Ethic and the Spirit of Capitalism*, Eng. Trans., Scribner; G. Allen, 1930, pp. 79-92: "Luther's Conception of the Calling."

4. I have used in the text the titles of books all published in the years 1920 to 1922: Lily Dougall and C. W. Emmet, *The Lord of Thought*, Doran; C. J. Cadoux, *Guidance of Christ for Today;* J. A. Hutton, *The Proposal of Jesus;* V. G. Simkhovitch, *Toward the Understanding of Jesus*, Macmillan. See also C. J. Cadoux, "The Politics of Jesus," *Congregational Quarterly*, xiv (1936) pp. 58-67.

5. *The Christian Register*, Feb. 2, 1922. See above, pp. 12 f.

6. Matt. 4:3-10 = Luke 4:3-12. Three false methods to fulfil his career are proposed to Jesus and rejected because he knew the better program for his life.

Another limitation of our records which vitiates so many modern attempts to conjecture motives in Jesus is their want of chronology. Beginning with the Temptation as an initial choice and trusting Mark's order as temporal rather than editorial scholars trace from stage to stage with great ingenuity the pattern of Jesus' plan. But as recent literary study shows us, the mere sequence of items in the gospels will not bear the weight of such reconstructions.

7. *Jesus, a New Biography,* by S. J. Case, Univ. of Chicago Press, 1927, Chapters V and VI.

8. A. Harnack wrote a special study of these passages, " 'Ich bin gekommen'; die ausdrücklichen Selbstzeugnisse Jesu über den Zweck seiner Sendung und seines Kommens," *Zeitschrift für Theologie und Kirche,* 22, 1912, 1 ff., and as a pendant to this, "Geschichte eines programmatischen Worts Jesu (Matt. 5,17) in der ältesten Kirche," in *Sitzungsberichte der Berliner Akademie der Wissenschaften,* 1912, i. 184 ff.

9. Mark 1:38 = Luke 4:43. Another example of the very early editorial introduction of the mission of Jesus is found in the *Fragments of an Unknown Gospel,* published by H. I. Bell in 1935, Oxford; British Museum. Under the influence of the synoptic "think not that I came," "Think not that I will accuse you to the Father" (John 5:45) becomes "Think not that I came to accuse you to my Father."

10. Mark 10:45; Mark 2:17 (= Matt. 9:13 = Luke 5:32); Matt. 5:17; Matt. 10:34 f.; Luke 12:49 f.; Luke 19:10 (cf. Matt. 18:11, omitted by the best authorities); Luke 9:56 (but the verse is omitted by good authorities); Matt. 15:24 (added to Mark 7:25). Do the last three passages indicate a tendency of scribes to add such sayings?

11. Rudolf Bultmann, *Die Erforschung der synoptischen Evangelien,* 1925, p. 32, now translated by F. C. Grant in *Form Criticism,* Willett, Clark, 1934, p. 59 f.

12. John 10:10; Gal. 3:13; Hebrews 12:2; Philippians 2:7; 2 Cor. 8:9; John 18:37; Mark 10:45.

13. "The more a man is united within himself, and interiorly simple, so much the more and deeper things doth he understand without labour, for he receiveth the light of understanding from on high." *The Imitation of Christ,* I.iii.3.

14. Cf. G. S. Duncan, *The Epistle of Paul to the Galatians,* Harper; Hodder; Musson, 1935. p. 74. Only once does a synoptic evangelist himself use "love" of Jesus' own attitude towards persons (Mark 10:21).

## CHAPTER VII

1. For the fundamentalist view that Jesus cannot be imitated and that his own religion is only in part an example for us, see J. G. Machen, *Christianity and Liberalism,* Macmillan, 1923, p. 92 ff.

2. On contemporary Jewish religious experience see especially in G. F. Moore's *Judaism in the First Centuries of the Christian Era* the section on Jewish Piety, and A. Büchler's *Types of Jewish-Palestinian Piety from 70 B.C.E. to 70 C.E.,* Oxford, 1922.

3. The viewpoint of the two preceding paragraphs was finely worked out by the late William Wallace Fenn, whose lectures on the theological method of Jesus will, it is hoped, be shortly published.

4. Klausner, *Jesus of Nazareth,* Eng. Trans., Macmillan, 1925, pp. 278 f. Cf. Luke 13:14 f.; 14:5. Even the illustration which Jesus used as an analogy was in other quarters a moot question, as is shown not only in the Talmud but in the fragmentary Zadokite work more nearly contemporary with Jesus: "If [an animal] falls into a pit or ditch, he shall not raise it on the sabbath."

5. Published by S. Schechter in *Documents of Jewish Sectaries,* Vol. I (1910). Cf. G. F. Moore, "The Covenanters of Damascus," *Harvard Theological Review,* iv (1911), 330-377; R. H. Charles, *Apocrypha and Pseudepigrapha of the Old Testament,* Oxford, 1913, ii, 785-834; Louis Ginzberg, *Eine unbekannte jüdische Sekte,* 1922.

6. C. G. Montefiore, *Some Elements of the Religious Teaching of Jesus,* Macmillan, 1910, pp. 40 f.

CHAP. VII *Notes*

7. F. C. Porter, *The Mind of Christ in Paul*, Scribner, 1930, pp. 14 f.

8. H. E. Luccock, *Jesus and the American Mind*, Abingdon Press, 1930, p. 40.

9. In arguing for the historicity of Jesus' miracles it has been said, "Jesus' faith is different from our faith in that it was the feeling and expression of a perfect filial consciousness. So strong was His sense of oneness with God—so vital, indeed, was the reality of that oneness—that He could perceive what the mind and will of God were, and could understand, therefore, what things can and must be done to fulfill that mind and that will. . . . We find in Jesus, therefore, a unique consciousness of the mind of God, together with a will perfectly in harmony with the will of God." Brown-Serman and Prichard, *What Did Jesus Think?* Macmillan, 1935, p. 148.

Similar unwarranted mind reading mars many otherwise scholarly works. As suggested earlier in this book, Harnack's *What is Christianity?* long imposed such imagined traits on an unsuspecting public.

10. D. B. Macdonald, *The Hebrew Literary Genius*, Princeton Univ. Press; Oxford, 1933, p. 9.

11. U. von Wilamowitz-Moellendorff, *Greek Historical Writing*, Oxford, 1908, p. 25.

12. J. Wellhausen, *Einleitung in die drei ersten Evangelien*, 2te Ausgabe, 1911, p. 104.

13. Gerhard Kittel in *Mysterium Christi*, English Edition, Longmans, 1930, p. 49.

# INDEX

Writers who are mentioned both in the text (with a quotation) and in the corresponding note (with reference to the source of the quotation) are indexed under the page of the quotation, not under the page of the note.

Abrahams, I., 67
Acts, Book of, 149, 176
*a fortiori,* 58 f., 101
Akiba, Rabbi, 64, 145
almsgiving, 106 f., 110, 164, 181
agrapha, 51, 104, 209
anachronisms, in art, 1-6; in literature, 10-14
analogy, 60, 101
angels, 78
anthropomorphism, 29, 161
apocalyptic, 26, 73-75, 87 f., 112 f., 170 f.
Aramaic, 51, 55, 81, 86
asceticism, 181
authority, quest for, 156
"authority," 70 f., 201

baptism of Jesus, 177, 179
Barton, B., 10 f., 195
*bath qol,* 178
Billerbeck, P., 67, 200, 204
Bonner, C., 202
Booth, H. K., 203
brotherhood of man, 93 f.

Brown-Serman, S., 9 f., 203, 211
Büchler, A., 210
Bultmann, R., 53, 209
Bundy, W. E., 155, 206 f.
Burkitt, F. C., 55

Cadoux, C. J., 130, 208
calling, 123
Carpenter, J. E., 205
Carver, T. N., 12 f., 131
Case, S. J., 132, 197
Charles, R. H., 210
Chesterton, G. K., 58
Christianity, argument from, 40, 69 f.
Coe, G. A., 204
Cooley, W. F., 208

Damascus sect, 50, 55, 171, 210
David, 63, 75
democracy, 94, 204
demons, 76, 78
Dibelius, M., 196
divorce and remarriage, 65, 66, 96 f.

[ 213 ]

## Index

Dodd, C. H., 198 f., 200
Dougall, L., 208
Duncan, G. S., 210

Easton, B. S., 206
Ecclesiasticus, 55
economic conditions of Jesus' life, 123 f., 140; economic views of Jesus, 12 ff.
Eliezer ben Jose, Rabbi, 63
Ellwood, C. A., 98-99, 111
Emmet, C. W., 208
eschatology, 127 f.; *see also* apocalyptic
Essenes, 66, 171
eudaemonism, 109
evolution, 82 f.
experience, religious, 155, 161, 186 f.

Fairbairn, A. M., 200
faith, the Christ of, 192 f.
fasting, 181
fatherhood of God, 9, 91, 92, 94, 204
Fenn, W. W., 206, 210
Fiebig, P., 67, 202
Fiske, G. W., 155
forgiveness, 105 f.
*Formgeschichte*, 198, 208 f.
Fourth Gospel, *see* John, Gospel of
Francis of Assisi, 143

Gamaliel, 59, 62
Ginzberg, L., 210
God, 76-78, 161, 187-189; substitute names for, 55 f.

Golden Rule, 64, 101, 108, 145
Gore, C., 11 f.
"gospel," 9
gospels, as preventive of modernization, 25-26, 31, 43 f.; as used in modernization, 28 f., 37; accuracy, 45 f., 86, 133; Jewishness, Chap. III.; unhellenic, 51
guidance, 183 f.
Guignebert, C., 208

Hadrian, 59
Harnack, A. von, 40, 104, 154, 198, 202, 209, 211
Hebrews, Epistle to, 21, 174 f.; Gospel according to, 104
Herford, R. T., 67
Herrmann, W., 104
Hillel, Rabbi, 64, 65, 145
historical imagination, 35 f.

"I came," 134-136, 143 f.
individual, worth of, 99, 102 f.
Inge, W. R., 203

Jacks, L. P., 133
Jewish vocabulary, 53-55
John, Gospel of, 20, 23, 30, 46, 57, 79, 133, 175
John the Baptist, 64, 65, 66, 171
Judaism, variety in, 50, 65, 169-171; Jesus' relation to, 145-147, 165-173
Justin Martyr, 23

Kant, I., 101
Kent, C. F., 204
King, G. B., 199

## Index

Kingdom of God, 9, 90 f., 98 f., 113
Kittel, G., 211
Klausner, J., 67, 167

language of the New Testament, 34 f.
Latham, H., 121
law, the Jewish, 146 f., 168, 184, 189 f., *see also* Judaism
love, 145, 150
Luccock, H. E., 196 f., 207, 211
Luke, Gospel of, 4, 21, 55 f., 137

Macdonald, D. B., 188 f.
Machen, J. G., 210
Macmurray, J., 207
"mammon," 54 f.
Mark, Gospel of, 70 f., 79-81, 208
Marmorstein, A., 200
martyrdom, 21 f.
Mathews, S., 89, 91-94, 202 f.
Matthew, Gospel of, 21, 22, 52 f., 71
Meir, Rabbi, 61
mentality of Jesus' environment, 43, 49 f.
Messiahship, 24 f., 130-132, 136, 151, 176, 184
miracles, 24 f., 79-81
modernization, cause of, 28-40; cure of, 42-45; in the gospels, 16-23
Moffatt, J., 114
Montefiore, C. G., 67, 109, 110, 172, 205

Moody, C. N., 208
Moore, G. F., 44, 62, 67, 200, 201, 203 f., 210
motives, in Jesus' teaching, 101-111, 143, 150 f.; of Jesus, 143, 149-151, 159
mysticism, 187 f.

non-resistance, 110 f., 205 f.

oaths, 66
objectivity in the Gospels, 28 f.
Old Testament, authorship, 75; fulfilment, 185; quotations, 47 f., 61
originality, 68-71
Otto, R., 44

parables, 35, 57 f., 160 f.; workers in vineyard, 100; prodigal son, 100; good Samaritan, 103, 116; talents or pounds, 13
Paul, 30, 61, 69, 137, 141, 152, 163, 175 f., 182
Peabody, F. G., 44, 89, 203
Pharisees, 65, 146, 149, 167, 171
Philo, 170
*Pirke Aboth,* 55
political interpretation of Jesus, 129
Porter, F. C., 176 f.
Powers, H. H., 116 f.
prayer, 164, 180
Prichard, H. A., 9 f., 203, 211
prophets of the Old Testament, 32, 60, 169, 172
purpose of Jesus, 120-149

# Index

Quakers, 173 f.

Rauschenbusch, W., 88, 89
religion of Jesus, Chap. VII.
Renan, E., 8
resurrection, 59-63, 65
Richardson, A., 207
Riddle, D. W., 196, 198

sabbath, 167
Sadducees, 62, 64
salvation, plan of, 125 f.
Samaritans, 62
Satan, 78
Schechter, S., 210
Schweitzer, A., 15, 42, 71 f., 74, 128
science, 73 f., 81 f.
Scott, E. F., 108, 113
scribes, life of, 124 f.
self-regarding motive, 102, 104 f., 149 f.
service, 102, 145
Shammai, Rabbi, 65 f.
Shema, 145
Simkhovitch, V. G., 129
sin, sense of, 181 f.; corporate, 182 f.
"single eye," 53 f.
Social Gospel, 88-94, 198
social groups, 97-99
social institutions, 95-97
social interrelation, 99-100
social motive, 101-111
social reform, 118 f., 128
social teaching of Jesus, Chap. V.
Socrates, 140

son of man, 135
Spengler, O., 15
Spirit, Holy, 20 f.
Starr, J., 201
submission, 141 f., 185 f.
success of Jesus, 136 f.
superlatives, in Jewish speech, 56 f.

taxation, 96
temptation, 131, 177
theism, 76-77
Thomas à Kempis, 148
Thoreau, H. D., 148
timelessness, 71 f.
"tittle," 57
transfiguration, 177 f.
Tyrrell, G., 198

uniqueness of Jesus, 34 f.
universality of Jesus, 33 f.

Weber, M., 208
Weinel, H., 201
Weiss, B., 207 f.
Weiss, J., 74
Wellhausen, J., 192
White, H. G. E., 196
Wilamowitz-Moellendorff, U. von, 191 f.
will of God, 126 f., 145, 153, 163
Workman, H. B., 195
Wrede, W., 128

Zadokites, *see* Damascus sect
zealots, 66, 171

www.ingramcontent.com/pod-product-compliance
Lightning Source LLC
Chambersburg PA
CBHW060602230426
43670CB00011B/1938